W9-BME-513

Anger

Books by May Sarton

Anger

A novel by
MAY SARTON

W · W · NORTON & COMPANY
New York   London

Copyright © 1982 by May Sarton

All rights reserved.

Published simultaneously in Canada by George J. McLeod Limited, Toronto.

Printed in the United States of America.

The text of this book is composed in Gael, with
display type set in Baskerville.
Manufacturing by The Haddon Craftsmen Inc.

First Edition

Library of Congress Cataloging in Publication Data

Sarton, May, 1912–
 Anger.

 I. Title.
PS3537.A832A73   1982   813'.52   82–7843

ISBN 0-393-01643-9   AACR2

W. W. Norton & Company, Inc. 500 Fifth Avenue, New York, N. Y. 10110
W. W. Norton & Company Ltd. 37 Great Russell Street, London WCIB 3NU

1 2 3 4 5 6 7 8 9 0

Envoi

I am the Prince
I am the lowly
I am the damned
I am the holy.
My hands are ten knives.
I am the dove
Whose wings are murder
My name is Love.

Charles Causley

Part I

Chapter I

Ned Fraser was forty and thought of himself as a "confirmed bachelor" when an unexpected event catapulted him into marriage. Until that morning when an old friend of his mother's dragged him to a musicale at the Copley Plaza, insisting that he simply had to hear Anna Lindstrom, Ned had considered himself a contented man with no wish to make radical changes in his life. His job was absorbing—he had recently become president of the State Street Trust—Boston was rich in music and for that he had a sustaining passion; and for the rest, he played court tennis three times a week, and belonged to the Tavern Club which provided him with good conversation with men of various capacities and interests. Women did not interest him very much, especially since a rather lackluster love affair had ended a few months earlier, leaving him with the conviction that sex was an overrated pleasure, at least if the woman involved had very little to offer beyond that. He and Janet had parted friends, and she was now engaged to a New York lawyer, much to Ned's relief. He intended to enjoy life, "fancy-free" as he put it, and to keep feeling out, except where Fonzi, his dachsund, was concerned.

But Ernesta Aldrich had been insistent and she was rather a dear, so Ned had agreed to meet her at the Copley Plaza and take her to lunch at the Ritz after the concert. There they were at eleven that Saturday morning, sitting uncomfortably on little gold chairs, when Anna Lindstrom and her accompanist walked out onto the stage. At once Ned sat up straight. What was it about her? She drank the audience in as though it were an elixir, smiling an open childlike smile that seemed to take in every single person to its warmth. Then as the applause died down, she became as grave as she had been a second before apparently lighthearted, and turned to her accompanist, waiting for absolute silence. All performers learn these tricks. In what way then was her way of meeting and captivating an audience unusual? Why, in fact, did Ned have the sensation in his stomach of rising too quickly in an elevator to the eightieth floor?

He took refuge from this alarming sensation in a cultivated detachment. He observed quite coolly the classical profile, the lift of her chin, just as she nodded to her accompanist to begin. He noted that a plain black dress as black as her hair, with a wide white ruffle at the throat, set off the whiteness of her skin, and the astonishing dark blue eyes. And once she had launched into a Fauré song he had heard many times before, he noted the purity and richness of her voice, a fine instrument used with the utmost mastery and tact.

Ned had been an aficionado of these French songs for years, had heard records of Povla Frijsch singing them and then of Maggie Teyte when he was in school, and more recently Janet Baker in London. As he listened to Anna Lindstrom he evoked them all and decided that Lindstrom had their advantage of musical intelligence plus a remarkable instrument, richer than either Teyte or Frijsch could summon. But at that point detachment fell away and he was given to this performer and to the music in a state of acute bliss.

"Aren't you glad you came?" Ernesta Aldrich whispered during the brief intermission after the first songs.

"Very," Ned murmured, "very glad."

"I told you you'd be surprised."

After the concert they decided to walk to the Ritz. It was after all a lovely day, and, as they walked, they discussed the performance.

"Interesting that she chose to open with the French songs and end with Mozart—most singers would have done it the other way around," Ernesta suggested.

"Yes, I suppose so. It seemed quite all right to me."

They had a table in the window, the table Ned Fraser always asked for and always got. He ordered martinis and clams on the half shell while Ernesta left for a few moments. The great white and gold room, its subdued elegance, and the Public Gardens below, a shimmer of just leafed-out trees over rich and varied parterres of tulips seemed extraordinarily beautiful, as though he had not seen them hundreds of times before. Even the napkin as he unfolded its ample damask folds seemed beautiful.

"Wake up," Ernesta said, laughing at him. "You're in a daze."

"Sorry," Ned rose and held her chair for her, "I was just thinking . . ."

"We'd better order. The waiter seems to be hovering around."

"Bay scallops, a salad, and coffee?"

That business accomplished, Ned looked across at Ernesta and smiled, "I must thank you for a memorable experience."

"I knew you'd be pleased. You are the only person I know who is as impassioned about music as I am, and I felt sure you would enjoy Anna Lindstrom."

Ernesta Aldrich, Ned thought, looked like everyone else in the room, well-bred, well-dressed, her gray hair rather too tightly curled, her distinguished face wrinkled, the dark eyes hooded and paling a little. But there was a twinkle in those eyes as though she imagined something of note was in the air.

"You're nearly forty, Ned. Aren't you ever going to marry?"

"Well," Ned cleared his throat, "I have no one in mind at the moment, but stranger things have happened, no doubt!" He found himself chortling for no apparent reason.

"What's so amusing?"

"I don't see myself as a husband. The idea struck me as humorous, I suppose." At this he laughed aloud.

"You think it's funny, but it seems to me pathetic."

"Pathetic?" Now Ned did wake up. "It's quite tiresome, Ernesta, to be looked on as some sort of freak if one has not wished to marry. I've had a rather good life so far, and if I may say so, a fairly useful one."

"Married to a bank! For me, there is pathos in that."

"But you don't really know, do you?" Ned was not in the mood for needling. He didn't want to be examined by this pitiless old lady like a beetle turned upside down, its legs waving in the air. "I read a lot. I go to concerts. I play court tennis. I have lots of friends—and my job is both demanding and fascinating. I like power and so far I've done rather well." But why make a thing of all this? Ned smiled then, "I'm never bored, Ernesta. Isn't that rather rare?"

"You are hopeless," Ernesta announced as the martinis arrived.

"No doubt." He asked the waiter to bring the clams right away.

Ernesta lifted her glass, daring him, he felt. "To love . . . and perhaps marriage," she said. "Sometimes anyway they go together, although not in French novels."

Ned lifted his glass, took a sip, and then set it down. "I don't know why I'm drinking to that. In my view neither love nor marriage implies happiness. Quite the contrary. I have never been as miserable over such long stretches of time as when I was in love."

"Ah, there we have it!"

"What have we got?"

"You've never found the right woman, Ned. It's as simple as that."

"Or as complicated as that. Let's change the subject, shall we?" He was not about to confide in Ernesta although that was clearly what was expected.

"Very well, you secretive man . . . I saw your mother at the Friday concert. She looks badly."

"She isn't well. She hasn't been well for years. She has simply not gotten over my father's death thirty years ago. As I need not tell you, she lives on not getting over it. It is her main occupation."

"You can be brutal, can't you?"

"Ernesta, do you remember those awful Christmases, when mother went to bed for the day, the blinds closed, and we tiptoed around, feeling it would be sinful to have any fun? We opened presents surreptitiously or indulged in some wild escapade just to break the pall?"

"It must have been ghastly, but after all, she's old now, and lonely."

"No doubt."

"I felt guilty when I saw her because I've neglected her myself lately, I fear."

"Exactly! Mother is a genius at making other people feel guilty. Don't let her do that to you, Ernesta!"

The clams came, and after a moment he went back to the subject, "I want to say something more about mother while I'm at it. She punished us and everyone else around because of her loss—and perhaps her guilt about that loss, who knows? We survived—it was the only way we could —by becoming stoics, by learning to shut our hearts against her grief. If I sound harsh, I can't help it. After all, Paul tried to commit suicide, you know."

"It's tragic," was her only comment.

"Is selfishness tragic? Is making the innocent pay for something for which they are not responsible, tragic? Is reaping what you have sown, tragic? I think of tragedy as having a larger dimension, a moral dimension somehow. Something has to be involved greater than the protagonists . . . " But sensing that he was being a trifle sententious, Ned held back and looked across at Ernesta, hesitant, "or don't you think so?"

"I don't know."

"I'll grant you that the loss of my father was tragic in itself. A car goes out of control and plunges over a bridge and a brilliant man dies, for no reason, by pure accident —that was a tragic circumstance. But what my mother made of that loss, the way she has used it, turned tragedy into something else. She chose to use it as the means of stunting her own growth and that of her children." Ned looked up, suddenly self-conscious, "I've said enough, too much maybe—more than I have said before to anyone." He gave a little cough. "I got all stirred up by that singer of yours. She has had a lamentable effect on me, I see."

"You have become rather loveable, old Ned."

"You're laughing at me."

Ernesta chuckled, "Yes, I am. One is permitted to laugh at loveable people, isn't one?" Ned was aware that he was being closely observed and finished his clams in silence. But when he lifted his eyes he caught hers, smiling.

"A penny for your thoughts," he said. "People rarely smile when they are thinking, but you were smiling, so I am curious."

"I was thinking about you."

"Then I'm glad you were smiling, not frowning." But her considering gaze made Ned a little nervous. He had given himself away and he regretted that he had done so.

"I was trying to imagine what went wrong with your love affairs, if you must know."

"I mustn't know," Ned smiled. "And you are not going to be told, so let's change the subject and order coffee. I have an appointment at two."

When the coffee came Ned knew he had to find out more about Anna Lindstrom. He had held off long enough, revealed too much about himself, out of sheer excitement, too keyed up to behave with his usual circumspection.

"Tell me what you know about our singer . . . I gather you have heard her before."

"You'd like to meet her," Ernesta teased. "You are smitten," she said with an air of triumph.

"That's going a bit far," Ned took a swallow of his demitasse and set it down. "I found her voice affecting, quite the most affecting voice in its range that I have heard since Kathleen Ferrier, and she only on records, alas. Like hers Anna Lindstrom's is not a cerebral voice. It has blood in it, if you know what I mean. But then the mezzosoprano often has that quality for me, less like a bird, more like a human being."

"And then she is quite a beauty. Black hair, dark blue eyes . . . "

"Irish?"

"No, half Italian, half Swedish. Her father was a doctor, her mother is of Italian descent and I think they live together somewhere in Brookline. Anna went to the conservatory here and then to Juilliard. What else can I tell you?"

"Why hasn't she been picked up by an opera company?"

"Oh, she has sung with the New England Opera Company—trust Sarah Caldwell to find a talent like that and know how to use it! I first heard her five years ago at a musicale at Fenway Court. I thought she was marvelous and went up to speak to her afterwards. She was quite radiant, so fresh and unspoiled. But of course she's come a long way since that day, makes concert appearances all over the place, sings as soloist with good orchestras, though not yet with the Boston Symphony."

"We'll have to do something about that," Ned said. "I'm on the Board, you know." He took a slim agenda out of his pocket and made a note. "I don't know that I want to meet her, but I'm certainly interested in hearing her sing again. You know, Ernesta, this kind of special gift, a little more than a talent, does not make its appearance every day. I am greatly in your debt."

"And I in yours for an elegant luncheon, dear Ned."

As they said goodbye on Newbury Street she told Ned she thought she would pay a little call on his mother.

Ned looked at his watch. "You'd better wait till tea time, she's lying down now until precisely four."

Chapter II

At thirty-four Anna knew that time was running out, and for any performer it is now or never. How she envied writers and painters who could always comfort themselves that the future would justify their long patience in the dark!

"Mamma," she cried out one day as she and her mother were taking a walk along the Fenway, "I feel as though I were under a stone in a graveyard, trying to push it up and shout, 'Listen! I'm here! I exist!' "

"Not so loud, Anna . . . that man just ahead of us turned around."

"What if he did? Is it a crime to wish to exist?"

"You don't want to be conspicuous, darling. It is not becoming."

"You sound like father. He was always trying to stop life from happening, wasn't he? He was always putting a damper on fire. It scared him almost to death. How did you ever live with him?" But already the moment of anger had passed and Anna slipped an arm through her mother's, and added more gently, "I'm sorry. I know he was great in his way, but it's not my way."

And so for a little while they walked along together and found the ducks waiting for Teresa to take a bag of bread crumbs out of her big handbag, and soon they were laugh-

ing as the greedy flock gathered and fought among themselves.

"Look at that poor one who never gets a chance. Let me
throw him something," Anna said. "Quick, Mamma!"

"Here, impatience!"

But the duck was frustrated again, swimming madly
toward the piece of bread, only to be pushed aside by
some stronger fellow.

"Damn it, I won't give up!" Anna said, but found the last
piece of bread had been taken.

"I guess you'll have to . . . for once." So they sat down
on a bench and rejoiced together in the balmy air, and the
bright leaves of the willow over their heads.

"Oh, Mamma, what would I do without you?" Anna
sighed. "Sometimes I wonder why I can't just sing for you
and for myself, sing for the sake of the music itself. Ambition is a curse."

"I know, but if you have a gift . . . and you know, Anna,
you do have an exceptional voice . . . you want it to be
used. Isn't that part of what ambition is all about? And
without ambition who would work as hard as you do? I just
wish you didn't have to take it so hard."

They sat for a few moments in silence.

"I feel driven all the time," Anna said then. "There is
never any peace. Except when I'm singing."

"Peace?" Teresa smiled.

"Don't tease me . . . besides it's almost time for my
lesson. We must get back. You know, Mamma, about
peace. Most of the time I feel like a swan muddling about
on land, heavy and no use to anyone, and then when I am
singing I become a swan who has glided into a pond and
swims, in its element, free . . . "

"Yes, and afterwards, the depression, the letdown," her
mother said, as they walked on toward the stand where
Anna would take a taxi to her lesson.

Anna realized it had been an unusual moment between
them. They were not always able to talk as intimately as

they did that morning. There were days when Anna was simply not there, absorbed in thoughts of her own. There were days when she felt as pent up as a wild animal in a cage, pacing about the apartment, days when the slightest frustration brought on a storm. So it had been since she was a child, "like a bolt of loose electricity" her father used to say. "You have to learn control."

Well, she had learned it, Anna thought, lifting her chin. Every one of her teachers had praised her control of her instrument. But control of herself? Anna wondered sometimes whether she would ever learn that. Punishment had never helped. That was her father's way, to tame the wild child by making her go to bed for the day, for instance. And what happened? She closed herself off against him. She used the punishment as some kind of battle, threw herself with fury into an act of defiance like painting a dragon on the wall!

For nearly a year Ned found himself on the periphery of the life of a prima donna, unable to get inside it. After a concert there were always flowers, other men's flowers as well as his own. Anna was away a great deal for concerts in Philadelphia or Cincinnati or Chicago. And when she was in Boston she was working hard on whatever music she would be singing soon.

She accepted the homage of the people who came to the Green Room, was merry, responsive, and charming, immensely charming, and she knew it. But if she was conscious of Ned as a person in his own right, he was not aware of it.

And for some time his invitations to dinner or a concert were refused on the grounds of her work. He had got quite accustomed to opening the envelope in her bold hand and reading, "Dear Mr. Fraser, I wish I could, but I am horribly tied up and obsessed by work these days. I'm truly sorry. The freesias are still delicious. Thank you again."

Ned tore up these notes and buried himself in the bank. But he could not get her out of his mind. Was she really as indifferent as she seemed? Had she for instance any idea who he was? And how could he make himself known? It seemed absurd that it was necessary. And it did not help that Ernesta, in whom he confided, was clearly delighted. "You've met your match, old Ned," she said.

"She doesn't even know who I am," he said miserably. "We're not even antagonists, Ernesta. I don't exist."

But Anna, amused and a little touched by the persistence of this unknown admirer, did discover through a chance remark at a dinner party in Louisburg Square who Ned Fraser was.

"Good heavens," she murmured, twisting a wine glass in her hand, "he seems so diffident, and," with a gentle laugh, "quite ordinary."

The gentleman on her left, who had not interested her until then, chuckled, and gave her an appraising glance. "You know him?"

"Oh, he sends flowers and comes to the Green Room . . . I don't *know* him. I just see him out of the corner of my eye on these occasions," she said, so offhandedly that her companion was silenced. But Anna came back to the subject when the dessert was being passed.

"Scrumptious," she said, serving herself to a large portion of a fluffy whipped cream and strawberry and chocolate creation. And then she asked Mr. Thornton to tell her what Ned Fraser was really like.

"He's reserved . . . people in his position can't afford not to be. A good fellow, though. We belong to the same club. He's affable enough, but he knows damn well who he is even though you, dear lady, do not. Anyone in the banking community would give a lot to know what goes on in that head."

"Is there nothing, then, but financial reports in that head?" Anna asked. She had in the last few moments withdrawn. She realized that she had been a little intrigued by Ned Fraser after all. But now she admonished herself to keep him at a distance. We live in different worlds, too different. We could never really be friends. For Anna, for all her temperament, for all her narcissism, was a realist, and had few illusions. She admired honesty in others and tried to be honest with herself.

"There must be something else if Ned sends you flowers," Mr. Thornton teased. "Perhaps you had better cultivate him and discover for yourself."

"No," Anna said, "I don't like the rich," and swallowed the last of her wine.

Mr. Thornton was clearly startled, for people usually don't say such things in the company they were in. He laughed, "Why not?"

"They take so much for granted, for one thing. And somehow or other they cannot escape arrogance . . . at least in my humble opinion."

"Aren't we all arrogant about one thing or another? You appear to be quite arrogant in taking Ned Fraser's flowers for granted."

"Touché!" And for the first time Anna gave Mr. Thornton her full attention. "But . . . but, you see, I have earned the applause, and the consideration, earned it a rather hard way. The flowers are thanks for something given."

"You don't see them then as asking for your attention . . . as hoping for a response?" Anna shook her head. She felt herself blushing. As usual she had gone too far, been too blunt, and aroused antagonism.

Mr. Thornton took in this embarassment. "As for Ned, I can tell you he works frightfully hard."

"I don't doubt that." Anna frowned, wondering whether to go on explaining herself or to let it drop. But

Mr. Thornton was clearly interested and she was about to speak when her neighbor on the right, whom she realized suddenly she had neglected, interrupted.

"What's all this about hard work?"

Dr. Springer, Anna remembered, was a brain surgeon at Massachusetts General. He was very alert, compact, with thin nervous hands which she had admired when they were introduced. "As far as I can see we are all work-aholics these days, and it's a very bad thing."

"Why?" Anna asked. "I can't imagine not working . . . work is my joy. It's what I'm all about. When I can't sing I'll commit suicide." She felt harassed and close to tears.

"Come now, if you lost your voice you'd still go on living, beautiful and alive as you are."

"I don't know that I would," Anna said. "What would you do if you lost your hands, beautiful and alive as they are?"

"I'd—I was going to say I'd devote myself to gardening, but without hands, you've got me."

"You see."

"Retirement does not necessarily mean becoming a cripple," he said a little testily.

"I just can't imagine life without singing—but you'd be amazed how long singers manage to go on. Lotte Lehmann had a whole new career teaching master classes until she was seventy or more! Of course she was the greatest . . ." Anna turned now to include Thornton, "All this began about money, strangely enough."

"Money and talent. Do they ever go together?" Dr. Springer asked with a teasing smile.

"Of course—why not?"

"You're changing your tune, Anna Lindstrom," Mr. Thornton said.

"No I'm not. A talent is no shelter. You can't take refuge in it. There is no safety in a talent because the more recognized and applauded you are, the greater the risk.

It doesn't matter whether you inherited millions or didn't. Don't you see?"

"There is, however, less urgency for the rich and perhaps a greater fear of failure," Dr. Springer said. "Without the necessity to earn, there is no immediate spur. It is easy, and perhaps far more pleasant, to settle for being an amateur, for not facing the competition. But do you still feel insecure, Miss Lindstrom? Your position, I should think, is unassailable. You seem so perfectly in control when one has the pleasure of hearing you in concert. Do you still feel unsafe as you suggest?"

"Unsafe? I'm terrified!"

"Come now, I don't believe you for a minute," Mr. Thornton said.

Anna turned back to the surgeon, "What nobody understands is that an artist, a performer has to prove herself over and over again. No one stands over you when you are operating and writes a review the next day pointing out that you fumbled, do they? In professional life outside the arts there are no critics in on every move you make. But we are targets. We are judged every time we open our mouths, sometimes by ignoramuses at that, and the public takes any critic's word as gospel truth. Of course I'm anxious. Of course I feel insecure. What performer doesn't?"

But just as things were getting interesting their hostess summoned them into the drawing room, its French windows opening to a balcony and the intimacy of Louisburg Square, and Anna, taking advantage of the spring evening, pushed one open and slipped through. At that moment she had a sudden desire to sing, to open her throat and launch into an aria. As always when she went out into society, she felt like a fish out of water. Either the conversation was trivial or if not, she plunged in too passionately, was too committed, too intense. Once more Anna's one wish was to escape.

Sensing someone at her back, she turned and greeted her host. "It's so lovely," she said, "the little square, the street lamps. I had to taste the air . . . What a marvelous place to live!"

"It used to be," Ambrose Upton said. "But the Hill is a disaster these days, dangerous at night. I used to walk everywhere, and often late at night, to smoke a cigar. Alice hates cigars. Now I can't do that." He led her gently back into the drawing room then, and Alice summoned her over to the sofa to sit beside her and poured her a demitasse.

"We are thrilled that you could come," she said. "Have you enjoyed yourself? You certainly charmed the gentlemen with whom you talked at the dinner table. Didn't she?" she added as Dr. Springer came to get his cup refilled.

"Didn't she what?" he smiled across at Anna.

"Charm you, of course."

Everyone was kind, but as usual Anna felt somehow like a household pet, something one patted and cajoled but who would never belong. Every society becomes a secret society to the outsider, she was thinking. But the truth was she was uncomfortable in any society, just as her father had been.

After Anna had left, early, with the excuse that she could not afford late nights—she was singing in Rochester three days later—Dr. Springer talked with Alice Upton about her.

"She's an interesting woman," he said. "There is something innocent about her, innocent and violent. She seems quite unspoiled so far. I expect she is on the brink of real fame and God knows what will happen to her then!"

Here Mr. Thornton joined them. "Where did you meet her, Alice? She's quite a lion, isn't she?"

"I suppose she is and I was thrilled when she accepted my invitation. We met at a luncheon an old friend of her mother's gave for her and I've known Mrs. Eliot for ages. We've been on various committees—to raise money for the Museum, for instance. Anna's mother is a very vital woman, Italian, as outspoken as her daughter. I expect that's where Anna gets it from. She married Dr. Lindstrom, you know, the neurologist who died some years ago. She has the most wonderful laugh—I'd walk a mile to hear Teresa laugh! After luncheon Anna very gracefully sang for us . . . I liked her a lot, quite apart from her marvelous voice. And so," Alice said, "it all seemed quite simple."

"I gather she doesn't like going out into society," Mr. Thornton said.

"We're not that exciting, are we?" Ambrose Upton said.

"But she has all the excitement she can use in her career . . . she doesn't want excitement," Dr. Springer said. "What does she want?"

"Recognition—the real thing. Fame." Ambrose Upton said instantly.

"And she doesn't have that? I seem to see her name rather often on concert programs these days," Dr. Springer said.

"Not quite," Thornton answered. "She's a tantalizing step from fame, but she's not a household word, not yet."

"She's never married?" Dr. Springer asked.

"Oh, she's absolutely single-minded about her art. I don't believe she'll ever marry." Alice said.

"I think she *has* to marry!" Dr. Springer said with such conviction it brought a smile.

"You?" Alice Upton teased.

"God forbid! I'm not out to marry a lion, I'm much too selfish." He laughed and then added more soberly, "Love, a passionate encounter, might provide the missing link, lift her right out of the almost-successful into the first rank."

"It's a physiological matter, you think?" Alice asked with a twinkle in her eye.

"In a way, yes."

And there the subject was dropped.

Chapter III

Five months had passed since Ned Fraser had lunched at the Ritz with Ernesta Aldrich. Anna had been away on concerts, had sung in San Francisco and at Wolf Trap, and Ned had gone to Europe for a month, to the music festival in Aix-en-Provence. Autumn was in the air and he felt exhilarated by the gold in the leaves, observing that the tulips of May had now changed to chrysanthemums in the borders, thinking that soon the swan boats would be put to bed for the winter. On an impulse he turned down toward the pond to see what was what.

And there under the bridge on the other side he saw the flash of a red coat, and a woman with black hair taking bread out of a paper bag to give to a flotilla of ducks.

"Anna!" he called, surprised by the sheer joy of seeing her into using her first name.

She did not smile as she lifted her head and looked across, wondering who had called, or whether she had dreamed that her name had been spoken by a man standing on the other side, but by then Ned had run up the stairs, across the bridge, and down to her, the pent up longing of months giving him wings.

"Did you fly?" she asked. "You were over there a second ago."

"Ned Fraser," he introduced himself as she seemed not to recognize who he was.

"Of course!"

"Imagine finding Anna Lindstrom here feeding the ducks!"

"I'm here quite often. My hairdresser is just around the corner." She gave him a curious glance and felt rather caught. Such an unexpected circumstance. Such a strange way to be confronted by Ned Fraser, too rich and too powerful, whom she had determined not to know.

"Well," Ned, fumbling for something to say, uttered, "it's autumn, a fine autumn day, isn't it?"

Anna burst into laughter. She couldn't help it. It was a crazy day, so brilliant.

"What's funny?"

"You are," she said, still laughing.

"Let's talk," he said, "come and sit down on a bench and observe the ducks and the swan boats . . . there must be a ride any minute."

"Take me on a ride!"

So they climbed the stairs and crossed the bridge, talking as they went, and down the other side to where the flat swan-boat barge waited, only a third full. They chose the back row and settled there.

"My mother used to take me on a swan-boat ride as a reward for going to the dentist," she said, "and then for an ice cream soda at Schrafft's, but I haven't been on one for twenty years! What fun!"

"It's the slowest form of locomotion ever invented and therefore the best, isn't it?" Ned asked. Inside the enormous artificial swan behind their bench a man sat and cycled them out in slow motion. It was amazingly comfortable, Anna thought, sitting there beside Ned Fraser and talking about little things, memories and pleasures. Here and there a gold leaf zigzagged down from a tree to the water. A flock of pigeons flew over and settled on the bank, waddling about on their pink feet.

"They are such ridiculous birds," Ned said, following her glance and the way she looked at them, wholly absorbed.

Seized as he had been by the lucky chance, Ned had forgotten his luncheon appointment at the Ritz. Now he took out his watch and frowned.

"Damn it, I have a luncheon appointment! Oh, how stupid!"

Anna began to giggle, aware that once on a swan boat there was no way to get off until the long journey up to one end of the pond, past the tiny magic island, and round to the other end, past the Victorian swan house on its wooden legs, had been completed.

"It's not funny," Ned said. "I'm going to be late."

"So you are," and Anna couldn't stop laughing at him, so prim suddenly and bankerish, caught on a swan boat. "Of course, you could jump off," she suggested.

"I could at that. But then I might fall in!"

"That would never do, would it?" she said solemnly. And then Ned laughed, too. He couldn't help it.

"Look," he said, "have dinner with me tonight . . . you must." And as he felt her hesitation, he reached over and took her hand in his and held it tightly. It seemed the most natural thing in the world.

Anna felt the warmth, the strength of that hand in hers like an injection of life into her veins. It all came over her there in the swan boat with great clarity that here was protection, an end to anxieties about money, a wonderfully warm and loving shelter. How could she refuse its gift?

"All right," she said.

And then they were silent, sitting a little stiffly, hand in hand on the last bench in the swan boat as it slowly, slowly reached the mooring and was made fast.

But when he had gone and she was hurrying, not to be late herself at the hairdresser, she was startled to realize what she had been thinking. What in the world made her imagine that Ned Fraser wanted to marry her? That he could have had any such thing in mind when he fastened his hand in hers with such strength? Besides, what made her think that she would ever want to marry him? "But I do," she answered herself. "The strange thing is that I do."

Why did she? How could she fall in love with a man she had never even talked to for more than a few minutes? And besides, did she want to marry? Why not a love affair? Why marry? She was stopped in these musings by the odd look an old woman gave her as she passed. Of course she had been talking to herself aloud! You're in a bad way, Anna, she admonished herself. But this time she did not speak aloud.

For once she, who told her mother everything, did not tell her about the swan boat ride, though she did mention quite casually that Ned Fraser was taking her out to dinner.

"I didn't know how to say no this time," she explained with a troubled look her mother caught instantly. "How does one say no on the telephone? It's an insidious instrument . . . and he interrupted me as I was going over the score. I got rattled."

Later when Anna came out, she remarked that her daughter was looking lovely.

Hours later Ned lay in bed wide awake. It had been an evening of precipitous, intimate exchanges. What was it about Anna that made it possible to talk about everything, no holds barred? God knows he was quite accustomed to the usual banter and teasing that takes place when a man and a woman are attracted to each other but have only recently met. But Anna would have none of that. So when he tried it by accusing her of putting him off for months, she answered with a straight look, those amazing blue eyes, suddenly black, "I was frightened."

"Of what?"

"I don't know. You tell me," she said, as though she really meant him to do so.

"Frightened of me? I was the one who had every reason to be frightened ... after all, you are Anna Lindstrom, my dear. And you have made that quite clear."

"Not because I am a little famous, but not very, but because your world and mine have so little in common, I suppose. Why begin a fugue you cannot sustain? Or play a part that is not in your range? "Yes," she said again, "I was not about to make a fool of myself."

"But you're not afraid now?"

Anna laughed, a loud laugh of real amusement, "I'm terrified!"

"That man at the next table is looking at you," Ned whispered.

"I can't help it if strangers recognize me. Do you mind?"

And Ned had the wit not to insist, for what he had minded was the indiscretion of her unself-conscious laughter in the solemn candlelit, velvet-curtained room of the Somerset Club. "Besides, everyone in this room, I imagine, recognizes *you*, and no doubt wonders where on earth you met that handsome woman and who in hell *she* is!" Then with a complete change of mood, she took a sip of the *Chateau Neuf du Pape*, swallowed it thoughtfully, and said, "That is a poem of a wine, Ned."

"You really live, don't you?" he had answered, "You appear to be aware of everything, the taste of the wine ... I did order something rather special but it is quite rare to have a good wine appreciated."

"Do I live? I sometimes think I don't ... or no more than a bird who lives to sing. But that's not it, either," she amended, again giving him that intent look he was beginning to hunger for like some food he had needed all his life and never eaten before and at the same time made

him extremely afraid of being found out, so he lowered his
eyes. "It is that everything matters too much."

And for the first time, they dared to be silent for a few
moments.

"Tell me about your childhood," she said then.

"Most of the time I was bored, bored or in revolt . . ."
It was strange, Ned thought, rehearsing the extraordinary
evening, how much he told Anna, partly because she listened so intently, and asked him such probing questions,
so it all poured out: the early childhood of summers in
Maine, of sailing wih his father, of reading aloud around
the fire, Dickens and Scott, Nils Holgersson. He told her
about his father's haunting voice, about his capacity for
fun . . . and then how all that was closed down by the
tragic death. He told of the years of imposed mourning,
"Dreadful," she kept murmuring, "dreadful for you."
More than once he saw the tears in her eyes.

"I took refuge in music," he told her. How all through
college he played the piano, went to the opera whenever
he could, concerts, played records, shut life out by im-
mersing himself in music. "So when I heard you sing," he
remembered saying . . . what a confession! How had he
dared say it? "it released something I had held back for
years. It was as though a whole world were opening inside
me, the world before my father died, the world where
anything is possible, where it is all right to feel . . ."

And she had reached over the table inviting a hand-
clasp.

"Dear Ned . . . that is a very great compliment."

Then she had talked about herself and her own childhood. "In a way we are at opposite ends," she had begun.
"You lost the parent you needed most, but I was able to
keep my mother. So for me everything opened when
everything for you closed." She told him about her father,
stern, unable to express anything except anger, a man of
tight control, "a sort of genius, they tell me, but all I saw
was the *gauleiter* at home. He never understood anything

about me, and of course I suffered for mother. You will love my mother," she had added.

And he had felt he must warn her that she would hate his.

"Yet there are similarities," she had gone on with whatever she was saying about herself, "I too took refuge in music, took refuge in a talent, I suppose."

The bottle of wine was finished, and they had come to lemon sherbert and coffee, when she finally asked, "Why did you become a banker?"

He remembered now how that question seemed to trouble the hours of intimacy, how it stuck out, and hurt a little.

"Laziness," he had answered, on the defensive. "Because of my grandfather the way was open. He had been president, you know, and I was a member of the tribe."

Ned felt more was demanded, more than he would have usually put into words. He was quite aware that for a person like Anna for whom art was possibly the only reality, the financial world must seem irrelevant, outside the pale. So after giving her one of his shy darting looks, he plunged in.

"Rather to my own surprise I found the Harvard Business School a very enlightened place, in some ways more enlightened than Harvard College appears to be."

"How do you mean?"

"More aware of what is going on in the world, more 'with it,' as they say." He smiled his quizzical smile. "Perhaps I shall disappoint you when I say that I find my job extremely interesting, that I am never bored . . . and then, as I was promoted rather quickly I began to understand the fascination of power, its risks. The financial world is full of risks and guesses. You stick your neck out."

"But you don't actually risk your neck, do you? The critics are not lying in wait with their machetes, are they?" He remembered Anna asking with an edge of antagonism in her voice.

"Of course they are. People can become very savage indeed when their income fluctuates. We handle hundreds of trusts, small and large. And these are often controlled by fairly eccentric wills, which the heirs are out to break. That sort of thing."

He had become aware that Anna's mood had changed and she was reacting, as he had feared she might, with a certain amount of hostility, so he tried teasing her a little by suggesting that there were just as many myths about the financial world as there were about artists and performers and their world. She had considered that statement quite some seconds, frowning, and then suggested that the banker had power and the artist never did.

"We are so vulnerable, Ned. All our lives, from concert to concert, from year to year, vulnerable to attack, vulnerable to our own frailties . . . a bad cold can mean ruin. A bad review can halt a career in mid-flight."

"You're exaggerating, surely . . ." but as soon as he had uttered the words Ned knew he had made a mistake.

The warm, compassionate look she had turned on him while he talked about his childhood blackened. Literally the very blue transparent eyes turned black. She appeared to be angry and close to tears at the same time.

"You talk about risks, but you are not risking your own body and soul . . . you are risking other people's money. So how can you know, how can you understand what I am talking about?" She had raised her voice and Ned felt horribly embarrassed, only wanting somehow to make her stop, to change the subject, to get out of the prickly pear tree. Luckily the waiter brought the check for him to sign, and Anna excused herself for a moment.

"I'll meet you in the hall," he murmured, rising as she did, watching her walk out of the room, apparently unconscious of the stares that followed her. But then he had thought, she must be used to that.

And he had not been surprised when old Mr. Goodspeed stopped him as he passed that table, and they chatted for a moment about this and that. Ned remembered how relieved he had felt to be back in his own world where nothing is said of any importance on social occasions, and one can feel safe.

The drive back to Brookline had been safe enough but Anna seemed withdrawn and this had the effect on Ned of making him feel rather cross as though he had been allowed into a secret garden and now found himself outside. He simply did not know what she expected of him or for that matter what he expected of himself.

Life for the past few years had been fairly plain sailing. Did he really want to risk whatever it was she had told him she risked at every performance? "Body and soul," she had said. It seemed a little melodramatic somehow. But when they reached the door of her mother's house he took her hand and held it hard in his for a moment as he had ages ago in the Public Gardens.

"Have dinner with me tomorrow night," he said, astonishing himself.

"Oh Ned, I can't."

"Why not?"

"Well . . . Oh, you know—next week maybe."

"I'm for seizing the moment. 'A little madness in the spring is wholesome even for the king.' "

"But it's autumn, Ned!"

"So it is. Have dinner with me tomorrow night."

And she had capitulated, on condition "that you take me somewhere simple where no one will recognize you . . . or me."

Having rehearsed the whole evening, Ned was still wide awake, impatient to be alive again, for he had felt so alive all that evening. Not at all his usual self, circumspect, an observer rather than a participant—and yet more himself than he had been for years. His comfortable shell had been broken open . . . but did he want that?

Chapter IV

"You appear to be falling in love, my child," Teresa said.

"Am I?" Anna who had been pacing about after breakfast turned suddenly. "Is that it? I feel quite ill, as a matter of fact." Then she sat down at the table and drank a third cup of coffee in one gulp. "What would happen if he asked me to marry him?"

Teresa looked across at her daughter, sitting there, her elbows on the table, her head in her hands, her dressing gown falling open to show the magnificent throat, and felt that Anna had changed in one night, had flowered, in fact, like a night-blooming cereus.

"I expect you would say yes."

"Stick my head in the noose?"

"You could do a lot worse, Anna."

"Oh, I know. That's the whole trouble!" And she knew that no more explanations were needed as they exchanged a smile and then burst into laughter. "He's a little too good to be true . . . and besides, we are as different as fire and water."

"Water could put fire out, you mean?"

"Oh," Anna said, clenching one hand, "I never thought of *that!*" It did give her pause. "But Ned can't really dim my fire, can he? Could he?" Anna got up and put her arms around Teresa's neck. "Give me some good advice, mother," she said, kissing the top of her mother's head. "Tell me what you really think."

"I think it's time you got married. I think Ned Fraser is a rather shy, sensitive creature and maybe it's time he got married, too. But for heaven's sake, daughter, don't rush into this."

"I know. How could I ever fit into his sort of life? And he has an awful mother, a monster of a mother from what he told me last night. How did I ever get into this? It's not what I want. Already I feel like a tiger in a cage!" She was pacing the room again, wanting as much to escape all this feeling that had her in its grip as to let it take her wherever she was destined to go, then sat down and looked her mother straight in the eye.

"Were you absolutely certain when you married father? Didn't you have any doubts?"

"I didn't have a career, Anna. I had no special talent. I think perhaps I felt the greater risk for me at that time would have been not to marry . . . I was not swept off my feet by your father, but I was flattered—he was already a very well-known physician—and, well, I did come to love him. Partly because he was such an orphan, so in need of tenderness, so bereft inside himself—and those awful depressions—he needed me, I felt."

"Yes," Anna sat down again. "Women are always falling for that . . . mothering their poor forlorn husbands. I could never mother Ned!"

"Ah, that's what you think, but tigers make very good mothers I have heard."

"Ned is formidable because he is so controlled, mother. Deep down inside I feel a coldness. Or perhaps an inability to give, to pay real attention to another human being."

"He seems very attentive to you, for heaven's sake . . . he has been sending flowers for a year and trying to get to know you."

"That's different. Besides I feel when he gets to know me—not the singer whose voice has touched him, but me the human being—he may not even like what he finds!"

"Well, he hasn't asked you to marry him yet. Give him time to know you. By the way, I don't want you to imagine that a temperament like yours is a flaw . . . not at all. It would be a shame if you let some old Bostonian take away your fresh response, your quick passionate reactions!"

Teresa did not often praise her daughter, but when she did, Anna listened. This time she heard praise as a warning. "You brought up a tiger not a mouse," she laughed. "And tigers don't change their stripes!" Anna looked at her watch. "Good heavens, it's after nine. I must go and practice!"

As usual talking with her mother had put everything in proportion again. She worked hard all morning, full of her own powers, hardly thinking of Ned. Work is the only fruitful passion, after all, she told herself. It's what I'm all about. Let no one try to take that security from her!

But in the five minutes after she had dressed that evening and was waiting for Ned—her mother had gone out to a concert—Anna experienced a storm of nerves. She went to the long mirror in the hall for the tenth time and looked not at her dress, a plain dark blue one with a dramatic white flaring collar, but at herself, the self that looked out from her eyes. "Don't forget who you are," she admonished the blue eyes, "Anna Lindstrom, the singer, not a thirty-four-year-old woman who feels inadequate half the time. Remember you are a tigress," she said, smiling at herself now, "not a mouse."

Ned seemed to sense her constraint and tension. He got lost trying to find the Italian restaurant—it turned out to have moved some blocks away—and clearly found it difficult to make small talk.

"I had a rotten day," he said quite crossly, as he manoeuvered the car into a small parking space. She sensed that he felt she was to blame.

It did not help that she was greeted effusively by the maitre d', "We are honored, Signora," who paid no atten-

tion to Ned's murmured, "a corner table, please," and led them to a table in the center of the room.
"No, not in the middle of the room," Anna said. And at last they were settled in a corner at the back. "He wanted to show me off," Anna whispered, smiling.
"Have you been here before?"
"No."
Ned then buried his nose in the menu, obviously still on edge.
"A cocktail, sir?"
"Of course. The same as last night?" he asked Anna and as she nodded, "two Johnny Walker Black on the rocks . . . and the wine list, please."
"So you had a rotten day, poor Ned." Anna was startled by hearing herself say "poor Ned" . . . so I am already mothering him, she thought. Don't do it. "I had a very good one."
"Tell me about it."
"I worked well, for an hour more than usual and in that hour I achieved something. It sounds like nothing, but I found a way to make a difficult transition sound easy. I've been trying to find the key for ages. You have to *think* your voice into doing things it may not want to . . . and this was a matter also of breathing." She was speaking intently and looking straight at Ned but she felt he was not there.
"I sat through a long director's meeting doodling," he said and laughed with what sounded like a trace of bitterness. "I'm afraid you are a bad influence," he now looked boldly at Anna, with unconcealed irritation.
"I don't see how I could be a good one," she was teasing him now and enjoying herself.
"Why not?"
And now she was serious. "You know, Ned, my work comes first for me. When I can sing I can be fully myself, give all my gifts, such as they are. I feel whole. Do you see?"

"I see," he said somberly. He took a swallow of Scotch and set the glass down. "And yet your voice is not a detached voice, singing or floating somewhere up in the air, it has blood in it. That's what is so moving . . . it has the earthly paradise in it, Anna."

"Does it, really?" She opened her eyes wide.

"You must have been in love many times."

"Oh," Anna gave her sudden fresh laugh, "I suppose so, now and then." But she was not in the mood to talk about that, the irrelevant past. "It's very mysterious, isn't it? I mean, what is a voice after all? An instrument, and if you have a voice, you become the servant of that instrument. You learn to guard it, to use it well . . . in a way to honor the gift, I suppose."

"I envy you," Ned said.

"What an admission! But Ned, you surely have a gift. Good heavens, you play around with millions of dollars, throwing flotillas of gold pieces into the air like a magician!"

And so at last the ice was broken between them. Ned clearly enjoyed ordering a good dinner and a good bottle of wine.

"You can alter the course of events, I suppose, as I never can," Anna went on.

They had not been able to recapture the intimacy and exhilaration of the evening before. And she had been quite mad to imagine that he would make a proposal . . . how foolish can I be? she asked herself. This is a cool character who doesn't want marriage with anyone. What do I see in him anyway, she asked herself, lifting her eyes to his face and by mistake meeting his probing glance full on.

"A penny for your thoughts," he said.

"Not worth a penny."

"I'm sorry I'm such a grouch . . . I don't know what's the matter with me."

But at that moment fettucini was placed before them

and the wine was poured. Anna fell to with enthusiasm.

"Mmmm," she murmured, "this is wonderful. Taste it, Ned. I bet you're hungry. I always feel cross and don't know why when I'm hungry!"

Ned obviously did feel better almost at once, and he seemed to enjoy watching Anna eating with such pleasure.

"Thank goodness you're not a woman who picks at her food and says she's on a diet!"

"I think this is simply delicious, don't you?" Anna caught his glance and laughed happily. "I love food!"

Ned gave a sigh of relief, then laughed with her and at her. "A devourer of life itself . . . that's what you seem to be."

"Is that bad?"

"It's marvelous, you goose!" Anna noted that a half glass of wine had loosened Ned up a little at last. "You said that I can change events as a banker. I can't really. I can only use events as they happen. I'm a manipulator I suppose one might say. It's quite disgusting, isn't it?" But somehow he seemed happy saying these things, and Anna observed his self-destructive joy with amazement.

"The arts, you see, change lives," he went on, smiling at her now, inviting her response.

"Do they? What lives have I changed, I wonder?" She was caught by the idea, but tossed it aside then. "No, it's not that, Ned. What the arts can do, it seems to me, is take people out into a pure world, a world outside time, and also untouched by the sweat and sordidness of ordinary life, give them a kind of peace, a sense of harmony—I don't know. I'm saying it badly."

"No you're not. You are frightfully articulate. It terrifies me," and he laughed, apparently pleased to be terrified. "What astonishes me is how simply you can talk about yourself, your voice, for instance, almost as though it were apart from you. You appraise it quite coolly and give yourself full credit."

"Am I so arrogant?"

"No, no, not arrogant. Just damnably clear-sighted. I didn't expect that somehow. It makes you quite formidable." He poured Anna another glass of wine and as he did so met her eyes full on.

"There's no hiding place down here," he said looking away. "And what, may I ask, are you thinking?"

"Oh," at this she became self-conscious and actually blushed. "I've forgotten. You puzzle me . . . shall I ever find you out?"

Ned laughed, "I shall do all I can to defend myself."

"Life's too short," she said. "Why defend yourself?"

"It's an old Bostonian characteristic, Anna. You must know that. Don't you have any defenses? I bet you do, only they're different."

They were so absorbed that neither had noticed a man standing waiting to catch their attention.

"Excuse me, but you are Anna Lindstrom, surely?"

Ned lifted his head and stared coldly at this interloper, but Anna gave him a ravishing smile and nodded.

"Would you be good enough to sign this card for my wife? I'm here on business. She would be thrilled."

"Of course . . . do you have a pen on you?"

"Will you by any chance be in concert near Chicago this year?"

"Not that I know now, alas."

Ned meanwhile summoned the waiter and buried himself in the menu. When the man finally withdrew Anna said, "What a nice man! He said he had heard me two years ago when I sang with the Chicago orchestra . . . "

"I thought him rather rude," Ned said coldly. "I can't see why you have to respond to such an intrusion."

Anna looked startled and dismayed, "But Ned, what could I do?"

"Tell him to go away."

"Antagonize a perfectly innocent person whose wife is an admirer? Could you do that? Yes, I suppose you could."

She looked across the table at this closed, self-conscious man for whom the surfaces meant so much. And whom, she saw suddenly, she had begun to love for all he was not, for all he had never had of ease and fun and openness.

"He didn't even introduce himself to me."

"You were buried in the menu, you spook," she said. "And why should he?"

"I dislike bad manners."

Anna sensed the spiral of anger rising in each of them. "Let's change the subject."

"Very well," he said grimly, "will you have dessert?"

"Zabaglione . . . " she said, tasting it with her voice as she uttered the word, "and coffee."

"Italian?"

"Of course."

Ned was not looking at her. He ordered and then there was silence. The waiters removed their plates. Anna's eyes roved round the room which had filled since their arrival. Ned drank his wine, twirling the glass absent-mindedly as he set it down as though he were formulating some equation, some financial ploy, way off somewhere— in his own world.

"Where are we?" she asked, to break the tension if it was possible. The trouble with burying irritation, she thought, is that it's hard to forget it and go on to something else.

"Nowhere," he answered, frowning. "The trouble is I want you uninterrupted, all to myself. Damn it, Anna, will you marry me?"

The question, put so bluntly, and in anger, took Anna by surprise and she laughed. "Good heavens, Ned, what a way to propose!" But the laughter ended as she met his shy, suddenly vulnerable eyes, and she laid her right hand open on the table for him to clasp, as he did with a strong triumphant grip.

"The answer is yes?"

Too sudden, too soon, some voice inside her was telling

her. Don't rush into it, her mother's voice whispered in her ear. They were all going up in flames, all her resolves.

"Of course," she said very quietly. "The answer, dear impossible Ned, is yes." But then Anna panicked. "I shouldn't have said it," she murmured, "we'll never get on. We're too different. You're marrying a tigress. You'll hate me half the time."

"And you'll hate me," Ned said cheerfully.

"Why should we get married then? Why ask for trouble?" but then Anna laughed again. And explained why. When she was growing up, still a small child, and her father still alive she used to escape to a neighbor's in Brookline where there was a family of girls, and when the servant over at the Lodges saw her sailing over on her bike, lickety split, she used to say "here comes trouble!"

"I bet she did," and Ned chuckled. "But why exactly were you trouble? Do tell me."

"Because I was always inventing dangerous games."

"Like what?"

"Oh, daring someone to climb a tree and jump off a high branch, things like that." And almost without a pause for breath Anna changed the subject, "Why did I say I would marry you? It's crazy—we hardly know each other!" And indeed Anna was terrified. She saw Ned as someone with a net he was about to fling about her, capture her, and she was not at all sure that she wanted to be captured. "Let's wait," she pleaded. Visions rose up in her mind of houses she would be expected to run, entertaining she would be expected to do, and she was suddenly close to tears.

Ned seemed unaware that her mood had changed. Of course it was mad to believe she could have fallen in love. And of course she hadn't. She had said yes to marrying a fortune, no doubt.

"We'll get married at Thanksgiving," Ned said firmly.

"No, we won't," she answered with a flash of lightning in her eyes. "I'm singing in Pittsburgh that weekend, the Bach *B-Minor Mass.*"

"Early in December then."

"Can it be a very small wedding?" she asked, suddenly meek.

"Of course. We're much too old for a big affair. That is for the innocents of twenty-one."

"I'm scared," Anna said, "and what will your mother think?" All the impossible things about marriage were swarming in her head . . . leaving her own mother . . . being interrupted in her work . . . being catapulted into a world she instinctively disliked.

"I couldn't care less what mother thinks. We just manage to tolerate each other, as it is."

Anna laughed, "And when I come on stage it will be open warfare?"

"Concealed under oceans of self-pity and perfect manners."

"Oh Ned . . . " She was fascinated by the dry tone with which he spoke of matters that usually were spoken of, if at all, with emotion. She decided that she had to be honest there and then, tell him the truth. "I'll tell you why I have doubts."

"You're not allowed to, you've said yes," he said briskly.

"The thing is I hate money. It makes me uncomfortable. You're too rich, Ned. That's one trouble, isn't it?"

"You're asking me?" he teased. "Very well, you shall have all the money you make and I shall have all the money I make and never the twain shall meet!"

"Be serious," Anna commanded.

"Well then, what's wrong about money? It's quite a useful commodity. It buys freedom from certain anxieties."

"Yes," Anna said, twirling her glass and frowning, "of course, but at a price. It also buys houses and cars and responsibilities and servants."

"Not any more . . . there aren't any servants, my mother tells me, and the only one I have is not even a servant in the old-fashioned sense of a loyal retainer, but instead a team of young men who come in like a whirlwind once a week, make an infernal noise, and leave the wastebaskets upside down on the beds."

"I shall feel I am going into a foreign land without knowing the language. Oh Ned," she said again, "let's wait till the New Year."

"Let's not. Think of all the fun we are going to have!"

"Are we?" She opened her eyes wide. "We aren't even lovers," she said. "It's just possible that one of us will feel shipwrecked on a desert island . . . imagine marrying someone you hardly know. It's crazy, Ned, absolutely crazy!" For what Anna was chiefly feeling at that moment was that the whole thing was unreal . . . that neither Ned nor she was really there, present in the flesh. It had become like a scene in a sophisticated comedy—and that was not something she could handle at all. And she who had held Ned with her eyes all through dinner now could not bring herself to look at him. She was overcome by shyness and terror.

"What made you propose? You were cross with that man, that's all. You wanted to assert yourself against . . . against . . . "

"Against what?"

"Me, I suppose." She lifted her head now and looked at Ned quite coldly.

"I proposed because I am madly in love with you, because I want you, Anna, more than I have ever wanted anything in my life. You must believe me."

Anna burst into laughter. She couldn't help it.

"What's funny?" Ned asked, obviously nettled by being put down just when he had made a declaration of passionate love.

"Dear Ned, has anyone ever uttered the words you just uttered in *that* tone of voice?"

"Did you want me to shout? The people at the next table are far too interested in whatever is going on as it is."

"I didn't want anything but—a little warmth perhaps."

They were saved at that moment by the waiter with the check. Why am I so attracted to him, Anna asked herself, observing his slightly flushed, closed face, the stern mouth, as he took his time to calculate the tip. She wanted to feel his cheekbones with her hand, and she realized that the warmth she had missed in his voice just now was inside her. It is very odd, she considered, but I have to admit that I am in love. The word, not uttered, but felt made her shiver. "It's so mysterious," she said aloud.

"Yes, it is," he said, smiling at her now the waiter had left. "But like bats who are blind, we are told, we have radar. I'm aware of every hair on your head, Anna," he whispered as he helped her on with her coat.

And once they were in the car, he drove around the corner to a side street, drew up to the curb, and kissed her. It was a long, sensitive, wise kiss, an exploratory kiss of discovery with a passionate truth in it at the end. And when he let her go Anna leaned back in her seat.

"Yes," she whispered, taking his hand in hers and holding it to her breast. "Yes, Ned."

Chapter V

All through that sleepless night the doubts flowed in. And by morning Anna was so busy writing a letter to Ned that she didn't hear her mother come in with breakfast on a tray.

"Are you all right, Anna?"

"Oh Mama," Anna turned her head from side to side like an animal in a yoke, "he asked me to marry him, and I said yes . . . but it's crazy. I'm not ready. I hardly know him." The tears she had held back all night poured down her cheeks. Teresa brought her a Kleenex, hugged her, and whispered,

"Take it easy. Write your letter. It's not a tragedy, darling."

"If I only knew," Anna murmured, "Mama, it is like entering a foreign country, not knowing the language . . . " Then she laughed, "He only asked me to marry him because he was angry!"

Teresa raised an eyebrow, "Well, drink your coffee. You've got to think this over, Anna. But from what I've seen lately you are certainly involved, if not in love."

"Oh, I'm in love, Mama!" Then she added quite coldly, "It's just that I can't imagine the future. I can't imagine what it will be like. I can't imagine being Ned's wife."

"Do you have to marry him?"

"Mama!"

"After all, you told me yourself that you would have love affairs but would probably not marry."

"That was five years ago, Mama, and you warned me that love affairs rarely last very long." She turned then and faced her mother, "I want this to last." Then she added very softly, "I want to feel safe."

"Oh dear," Teresa smiled, "marriage is not exactly safety, you must know that."

"I'm too old for a love affair."

"Nonsense," Teresa went to the door, "I'm going to leave you alone to sort yourself out." But at the door she hesitated, smiled, reminded Anna that her father used to say "be as wise as the serpent and as gentle as the dove".

"Impossible . . . I'm a tigress. You tell me so yourself. And besides what did Father know about love?"

Teresa gently closed the door.

How empty the room felt after her mother had gone! Acute loneliness took her place. Anna swallowed the cup of coffee, then sat at her desk for a long time, rocking herself, her arms clasped around her, holding herself together. Then she wrote.

"Dear Ned, You have been thinking about me for a long time, but I have not been aware of you until a few days ago. You have made me feel more than I have for years. I look at your face and want to touch you. I look at your hands and want to hold them very hard and fast in mine. I look at your mouth . . . " here Anna stopped for a moment, dizzy with the longing for more of those kisses. Why hesitate? " . . . and need your kisses. I love you. But, Ned, we hardly know each other. We have talked so much, we have given each other our lives—that has been wonderful, all the doors open suddenly, such a deep real exchange. And yet we don't *know* each other. Can you understand?" And she signed it simply "Anna," not as she had wanted impulsively to do, "Your Anna." Not yet.

The letter was delivered to Ned's office by messenger.

For he was sure to call and it was absolutely necessary that he read it first.

At six that evening Ned called, "Anna, it's been a wild day here and I'm only just home. I didn't want to call you from the office."

Anna was silent. She waited because she was frozen with anxiety. "Did my letter reach you?" she managed to utter.

"Yes. Anna, will you come and spend the weekend with me in Beverly? I have a house near the shore there." It was said in such a brisk assured voice that Anna couldn't help laughing.

"The president of the State Street Trust has made a decision!"

"Don't tease me. Please come."

"That's the day after tomorrow," for a second she hesitated. "All right."

"Good. I'll pick you up on Friday at half-past five. Wear old clothes."

When she put the phone down, Anna realized that two days would be a very long time. And then she smiled. This amazing man had not uttered a word of love. But he had, she admitted with admiration, answered her letter with action, the one necessary action. And swept her quite neatly and decisively off her feet.

But if she had been nervous about being in his territory in "a foreign land" as she had said to her mother, Anna was amazed to find that she felt at home from the moment they walked into the small cosy house and she helped Ned stow food away. The gardener had turned the heat up so it was not the chill house she had dreaded, and besides that it was full of charm, old blue and white china, copper jugs on a side table, some old-fashioned water colors of the shore, that looked like Sargents.

"Here, you arrange them," Ned said, handing her a box of yellow roses, "There's a tall Steuben glass somewhere. . . . Oh, I know, in the corner cupboard there . . . you'll find it."

He was being efficient and quick. She liked the way he did things, liked it that they had crossed the threshold in an impersonal hurry to get sorted out. For now they were alone really for the first time—except on the swan boat! —it was healthy to have a lot to do before the momentous fact that they *were* alone could overwhelm.

"There," Ned said coming into the living room, "I'll light the fire and then show you your room—when you come down there'll be a drink. What shall it be?"

"Scotch, please, with a little water," Anna said as she brought the roses in and set them on a small table. "Oh smell, Ned! Isn't that delicious?" As he bent down to smell, Anna's heart missed a beat as a rush of longing to kiss the back of his neck took hold of her, but she didn't. It was a little like being in the middle of a piece of music that must be allowed to continue without interruption until . . . until . . .

"Well, come along then," Ned said, picking up her suitcase, "Hey, what have you got in here? It's heavy as lead."

"Scores, Ned. You said there was a piano—at the last minute I put in some songs!"

"Wonderful . . . " and then without further ado he was running up the stairs, and leading Anna into a small room with yellow walls and a comfortable looking small bed. "There's a bathroom," Ned said, opening a door. "I'm afraid it's rather Spartan, though. Paul and I lived here for a while . . . not very feminine, is it?" He smiled rather shyly. "I can't believe you're here." Something though was troubling him. And as he turned at the door on his way out, he murmured, "My room is better."

"In what way?"

"It has a double bed," he said, running down the stairs leaving Anna laughing in spite of herself at how little Ned could express, at how terribly self-contained he was even on this momentous occasion. But will it be a bridal night, she was wondering? Or will it turn out to be a huge mistake? What did it matter? For the moment Anna felt happy, excited and happy, and, she realized, unexpectedly at ease.

Somehow coming into this house had broken a spell. It didn't feel like a foreign country, after all, and when she went down and found Ned mixing a salad in the kitchen, he did not feel like a stranger.

"Italian peppers, you marvelous man!" She seized a strip of one from the bowl and chewed it. "What are we having for supper?"

"The great American meal . . . steak, baked potato, salad."

"And ice cream?"

"How did you guess?"

And they laughed. Why was it so funny? Not really, but it was such a relief to be able to laugh and to be at ease. And then at last Anna ran a finger along Ned's cheekbone and along his mouth. "I've wanted to do that," she murmured. She felt the tremor under the skin—sensed Ned's acute sensitivity to her touch.

"Come and have a drink," he said crisply. "We have lots to talk about."

And there they were, sitting side by side on the sofa by the fire, forgetting to drink their drinks on the table in front of them because Ned was holding Anna's hand, hard and fast. "I'll never let you go," he said. "Never."

"Dangerous statement. Someday you might want to get rid of me."

"Maybe I made a mistake," Ned sat up straight. Whatever was this about, Anna wondered. "I left Fonzi with a friend."

"Who's Fonzi?"

"My dog. He's a dachshund. I'm sure I've told you about him."

Anna took a sip of her drink. "Why didn't you bring him?" At this question, Ned too swallowed a mouthful of Scotch, began to laugh, and choked on it. When he had recovered he said,

"Because he sleeps on the bed. And . . . " Ned hesitated, "he might be jealous."

"Well, of course a bite in the night might be a little startling," Anna responded very gravely. But it was too much and when she began to laugh she laughed till tears rolled down her cheeks and Ned was doubled over. "Oh Ned, you dear funny creature!"

"Sooner or later you'll meet Fonzi. He's really a very affectionate fellow," he said when he could speak.

"I'm sure he is."

"Tomorrow we'll go for a walk along the beach . . . " But Anna was thinking tomorrow is an eternity away and . . .

Ned caught her withdrawal, let go her hand and took a swallow of his drink. "When you go away like that I feel left out. Look at me," he commanded.

But Anna put her face in her hands.

"Come back," he implored.

"I've not gone away. I'm just thinking . . . You've had time to imagine me for over a year, to imagine this. I haven't. For me these past days have been an explosion that I wasn't prepared for and haven't had time to understand." She lifted her head and examined him almost coldly. Did she really want to let him into her inmost self? But there was something in her that wanted to break open that closed, self-contained arrogant face, and again she couldn't help running a finger along his cheek.

This time Ned turned, took her in his arms and kissed her fiercely, possessively, and would not let her go till they were both out of breath.

"Imagine that!" Ned said with droll matter-of-factness. Then he got up and pulled Anna to her feet. "Let's go to bed."

"Without any supper?"

"We'll make love till we're ravenous. Then we'll eat."

"Ned!" Anna said, but she was pulled along. She felt the tide rising beyond either their ability or wish to hold it back. And she knew almost coldly that they had to get it over, to find out where they were, who they were, together.

But that was not exactly what happened. For there in the big bed in Ned's room, she experienced the jolting force of his need in darkness. His hard chest against her soft breasts hurt a little. Never had a man penetrated her so deeply, so that at one moment she gasped.

"I'm hurting you."

"No, don't go."

"Oh Anna, Anna!" He held her gently then and rocked her back and forth still deeply inside her, till the last spasm came and went. Then he gave a deep sigh, "It's good to let go."

Anna was now living at such speed, hurtling among the stars, she felt, that her mind would not stop thinking, and at the same time she was wholly relaxed, one breast cupped in Ned's hand. She was thinking with her whole body, still tingling, still wonderfully alive down to her toes. But at the same time she pondered the curious fact that this most intimate and personal of acts between human beings was, when fully consummated, actually quite impersonal. It was not Ned so much of whom she had been aware as of their being part together of a primal scene, of being as she put it as she lay there, united in some strange way with the universe itself rather than with each other. To go so far out with another person was a little frightening, now that she was coming back to the dark bedroom, alone. "Ned," she whispered, and realized then that he was asleep.

How could he be asleep? It seemed astonishing, but she supposed that that "letting go" as he had put it, had given him in the end this bliss, perhaps, of unconsciousness. He did not, as she did, have to be aware, for the stronger the emotion involved, the greater her need to understand what exactly was happening. So she lay there wide awake, until Ned suddenly sat up.

"What time is it?"

"God knows, my darling. You've been asleep."

"Well, we'd better get ourselves something to eat!"

"Put on the light, I want to see you."

It seemed to Anna the most natural of requests but its effect on Ned was unexpected. "No," he said, "I'm not ready," and he disappeared into the bathroom. When he came out and turned on the light he was in pajamas and Anna instinctively pulled the sheet up to her chin.

"Get into a dressing gown or something and I'll run down and start things . . . aren't you ravenous?"

"Come here, you oafish character," she commanded. And he stood there by the bed looking down at her with a rather quizzical expression.

"Ned, are you there?"

"Yes."

"Do you love me?"

"What do you think?"

And before she could answer he had turned away and run down the stairs. Was it possible that he couldn't say it?

"What a splendid sight!" Ned said when she came down after a few moments in a bright red dressing gown ruffled at the throat. "The prima donna!"

"Hardly! Prima donnas do not eat supper at after nine in a bathrobe."

"Is that a bathrobe?" he teased. "It looks like something

meant for a chaise longue . . . Stretch out here by the fire and I'll open the champagne . . . steak will only take a few minutes. Rare, I trust?"

"Medium rare."

Anna felt she was floating, not quite touching the ground, a little unreal. She didn't stretch out, she sat on the chaise looking at the fire, or rather the ashes of the fire, a few bits of the log still glowing. Then he was standing, his back to the fire, lifting a glass of champagne, "To us. To Anna Lindstrom . . . dare I say, Anna Lindstrom Fraser?"

Anna lifted her glass, "To us . . . but I can't give up my name, Ned."

"No, I suppose you can't."

"I have to be Anna Lindstrom whatever happens." There was a sharp edge in her voice, but she couldn't help it. "We have to talk, Ned."

"Do we? Don't spoil it, Anna . . . let's have our dinner in peace."

"Without a word?"

"You know what I mean."

Would Ned ever be able to talk about his feelings, would he ever open his heart to her, Anna wondered when they set out the next morning to walk the beach in a rather bleak fog?

"I feel like running," Ned said, letting go of her hand after a few minutes of walking in step with her. And off he went, trim and sprightly on his elegant long legs, until he was just a lean shadow far down the beach. Anna was glad to be alone, to listen to the gentle roar of the waves, coming in at a slow tempo for the tide was ebbing, smelling the iodine of the seaweed scattered about, stooping to pick up a broken sand dollar and knowing that whatever the hazards, despite the huge temperamental rift that was becoming clear to her now, she would have to marry Ned. At some point reason ceases to operate. I'm in for it, she thought . . . marriage! And she had to laugh at herself for she felt, at the second of realizing that, like a porcupine with its quills rising.

And later that afternoon after Anna had taken a nap, they sat by the fire, drinking tea, she took the bull by the horns.

"I'm not quite sure what is happening to us, Ned. On one level everything is sort of overwhelming, but on another, I have no idea what you are feeling inside yourself. Do you want to back out maybe?

"Good heavens, Anna, whatever makes you ask that?" He sounded quite cross. "Maybe you're the one who wants to back out. Maybe that's what that question was really all about."

"Please don't shut yourself off, Ned." Anna took a deep breath. "It's just that we are such different people . . . I mean, words are very important to me. I need to say that I love you . . . and I do. But I also need to hear you say it. Do you realize that all through last night you never said it?"

"But surely you must know that I do—after last night!"

"You never use an endearment. It seems so strange . . ."

"I can't help it, Anna. With me such things go too deep for words, I guess."

"I just don't believe that!" Anna felt her quills rising. She was close to anger or to tears. "It's mean and inhuman. It's ungenerous."

"Anything else?" Ned asked with heavy irony.

"I just don't understand," Anna said and got up and went to the window, looking out at the fading light and a chickadee busily pecking at the seeds in the hemlock.

"I've asked you to marry me . . . is that mean, inhuman, ungenerous?"

"I can't see what's making you so cross," she said, still

looking out, her back turned to him.

"It's you who are cross, my dear. I appear to enrage you because I can't and don't want to sound like a greeting card."

But this was too much and Anna whirled around and rushed at him. Ned, startled no doubt by this sudden eruption of violence, got to his feet and managed to grasp her hands before she could hit him.

"Let me go!" she said.

He let her go, but he was frozen with dismay, and looked it.

"I'm sorry, Ned," Anna said coldly. "But I can't take that sort of nasty cut without reacting violently and you might as well know it."

"I think I'll go for a walk," he said, going out into the hall to find a coat.

"Oh Ned, please stay. We've got to talk."

"It's become too dangerous. I find physical assault repulsive."

"Darling, I'm sorry . . . " she followed him into the hall and gently took his coat from him and hung it up. "Please . . . "

Ned stood there, his head bent, looking suddenly so at a loss, so forlorn that Anna impulsively leaned over and kissed him. "You are such a strange man," she said then, "But I do love you—that's why you make me so angry, I suppose."

"I just feel awful, sick," he said. "Let's sit down." On the sofa Ned leaned his head back and closed his eyes. Anna reached over and took his ice-cold hand into both of hers.

"I can't understand," he said after a moment. "One minute you're in a fury and the next you are telling me you love me. I can't move that fast from one mood to another, Anna."

"People in love are vulnerable, Ned, and easily hurt. And," she went on very quietly, "people react differently to being hurt. I react with anger. You withdraw."

"Mmmmmm."

"But it's not fatal. It's just that we are very different."

"Fire and ice," Ned said and smiled for the first time.

"Maybe." Then Anna met his eyes, "But you're not ice. You're fire, but it's under ice . . . it's locked in." And indeed when she was lying down earlier that afternoon in the limbo between sleep and waking, when images float up from the subconscious, she had had a vision of Ned as a swimmer under water, but there was a thick layer of ice on the surface. It was a nightmarish vision. And she had pushed it aside and gotten up.

Now it came back. Anna looked at Ned with more love than she had perhaps ever felt before for a man. And she told herself that surely tenderness and true love would melt the ice and set the swimmer free. Her moment of anger had forced her to go deeper, to be with Ned in a new way. That was strange.

Part II

Chapter I

The scene on an October night two years later was tranquil. Ned was sitting with his feet up leafing through a French economist's analysis of the world recession. But although everything was still there was an air of expectancy about him, and when he heard the clock strike eleven, he got up, put another log on the fire, and stood for a moment surveying the large room like a critic. In the window a small table had been set up with a plate of cold chicken, salad, a basket of French bread, two champagne glasses, and two chairs. Within a half-hour Anna would be home after singing with the Boston Symphoney in Mahler's *Lied von der Erde*. For once Ned had not accompanied her. He had had to attend a dinner for a visiting director of a West German bank. Anna had not liked that at all, "For once, when I am singing in Boston, Ned, it's not fair."

"I wanted to come. You must know that."

"Two years ago you would have managed it somehow." Her eyes were bright with tears. But after two years of marriage to this emotional woman, tears irritated Ned, and he had not even wished her luck as she swept out. Now, remembering that exit and dreading her return, he went into the bedroom and gathered Fonzi, their dachshund, up from his basket and brought him into the living room.

"I'll take you for a walk after she has her supper," he promised, as Fonzi stood there, wagging his long tail with furious anticipation. "Later, Fonzi." The biddable animal lay down on the hearth rug, his nose on his paws, one eye following Ned as he lit a cigarette and sat down again, but did not pick up his book. Instead he looked around the room measuring its discreet beauty and order against the disorder and chaos of the life he and his wife were living inside it.

The room was gray and oyster white, the carpeting thick velvety white, the walls pale gray to set off the two small Vuillard's on either side of the fireplace. Over the gray and white striped sofa opposite Ned had hung a Bonnard, the Mediterranean very blue seen over a terrace and the tops of trees. He never tired of looking at it. Anna and he had agreed from the start that this was to be their own atmosphere, not that of his mother's house, dark and cluttered with objets d'art and eighteenth-century English furniture, nor that of her mother's, for that matter, inhabited by heavy old Swedish furniture with some Italian pieces mixed in. How he had admired Anna's forthright refusal of various things his mother wanted to bestow! "It doesn't feel like me," she had said more than once. "It's too grand, Mrs. Fraser."

And to Ned she had apologized, "But we can't live her life, Ned. Even if she is hurt. I can't help that!"

"You're so fierce about it."

"I'm fierce because it's so hard to be definite and not give in, can't you see?"

At that time everything that now irritated Ned had seemed rather wonderful, including Anna's blunt honesty.

Fonzi interrupted these thoughts by barking excitedly. How did he know? For it was some minutes before he heard Anna's key in the lock. She came in, flushed, her arms filled with roses, and went right past Ned to the kitchen to put them in water. Ned picked up three red ones that had fallen and followed her in a strange silence, for Anna had not uttered a word and neither had he.

"Here, you dropped these . . . some fellow's heart's blood, no doubt!" Ned laid them on the counter on top of the others.

"I've got to change first." He helped her off with her coat. "Hang it up, will you?"

And she left him there, his arms filled with purple velvet and sable, stroking the fur absent-mindedly. Then he went to the hall closet and hung the coat up. Impossible to tell yet what her mood might be. But his own ancient Burberry hanging beside her coat gave him an idea. He slipped it on, took Fonzi's leash, and as the excited barks rang out, knocked on the bedroom door, "I'm taking Fonzi for a walk while you change, Anna."

"All right," her voice sounded quite cheerful. "That's a good idea."

When he got back a half-hour later, Anna was waiting, stretched out on the sofa in a dressing gown. Fonzi ran to her, his tail nearly wagging itself off and she sat up and took him onto her lap. "Oh my Fonzi . . . I thought you'd never come back. I'm starving, Ned."

"Well, let's eat. Everything's ready, as you see."

"Kind of you," she said, taking her place and snatching a piece of celery, devouring it, entirely absorbed in crunching it up.

"Well," Ned asked, "how did it go?"

"You don't really want to know, do you?"

"As you please."

For a second she met his eyes and wondered how to stop the spiral of irritation which they both knew was already starting to build up.

"I did well, Ned. I think I did, although that maddening man changed the tempo in the *Abschied* . . . slowed it down and me down, so twice I was nearly out of breath.

I got the silence, though, at the end. There must have been thirty seconds of silence before the applause."

"Bravo!"

"If you could only say that with some warmth!" The letdown from the heat of the concert hall, the standing ovation, the whole atmosphere she had come from, was impossible to convey to this man, her husband, who could say bravo in the tone one might use to tell a dog to lie down.

"You know I can't. I can't shout and wave my arms sitting opposite you at a table. What do you expect?"

This Anna chose to ignore. She was eating her cold chicken with gusto.

"You *are* hungry."

"I've been running a marathon . . . you never have understood what a performance like this takes out of me."

"Nor perhaps what the exhilaration is of holding an audience spellbound for an hour. My evening was, it must be granted, rather a different kettle of fish."

"There was a lot of coughing and I wanted to kill them!"

Ned couldn't help smiling at the absurdity of it, the fury of Anna's feelings.

"I know I'm ridiculous," as usual she felt put down, no longer able to hold on to her triumph, watching it taken from her as Ned always managed to do in one way or another. "I ought to be shot at dawn."

"That is a slight exaggeration, my dear."

"Why is it, Ned, that you can only use an endearment ironically?" Anna knew that she was asking for trouble but something in her wanted trouble, wanted anything that could bring her down from the high tension wire of the performance, get rid of the tension. She pushed her plate aside.

"Have some more chicken, Anna."

"No thanks."

"We forgot the champagne but there is dessert. Felicia

made trifle . . . we can have some now."

They went out companionably to the kitchen where Anna served the trifle and licked the spoon, and Ned, after a nerve-wracking struggle, got the champagne open. The cork flew up to the ceiling, just missing a porcelain duck on a high shelf.

"Wow, that was close!" she said, delighted. "Now give me a kiss." His lips just brushed her cheek. "A butterfly could not do it more passionately," she teased.

"I hope you notice it's the real McCoy . . . *Cordon Bleu.*"

"Yes, I noticed. We are being extravagant."

"It's not every day that Anna Lindstrom sings with the Boston Symphony."

"It's not every mezzo-soprano who has a husband with influence."

"Don't hold it against me."

"Don't spoil it. Fonzi is waiting to lick the plates!"

They sat down. Anna lifted her glass without lifting her eyes, took a swallow and put the glass down. "There's nothing like it, is there?" She was thinking that the only safe area now between her and Ned was food and drink. Almost anything else they might talk of—except Fonzi of course—had pain in it or had the capacity to make pain surface. And all too often the pain took the form of anger. She looked at him then, trying to read his closed face as he tasted the trifle.

"Tell me about your German banker."

"It wouldn't interest you."

At this she laughed. "How do you know if you never try? Give me the benefit of the doubt! What did he look like?"

"I really can't remember." And it was possible, she thought, that this was the truth. The German banker was simply a counter in a game for Ned. "But he was extremely civil at any rate. The Germans are in a peculiar position because of our high interest rates. Also the dollar has not really rallied. They had everything to gain from a weak dollar in some ways, and in others, it is damaging because of trade."

"It sounds like a maze. Don't you get terrified at times that it is a maze and you will all finally get lost trying to find the center?" But even as she spoke Anna knew that this kind of teasing simply bored Ned. "I know I am idiotic," she said. "After all I never went to college."

"You had better things to do." It was a perfunctory response. He yawned then, "It's really been rather a long evening, Anna. Let's go to bed."

"We never talk about anything real. What has happened to us?" Anna got up and took the dishes into the kitchen, followed by Fonzi who now gave a sharp bark of distress. "Oh Fonzi, my darling, I quite forgot you," she said, setting the plate down for him to lick. "It's not every dog who eats off a Copenhagen plate!" And to Ned who had followed her with the glasses and the bottle, still half full, "Do you remember when we bought these?"

"I remember the salesman fell all over himself when he recognized you!"

"And how you hated that! Yes, of course you remember," Anna said bitterly and on a rising inflection.

Ned winced visibly. "We're not going to have a scene," he said coldly.

"No, why should we? There's nothing left to have a scene about."

But Ned didn't answer for he had gone into the bathroom and closed the door. While he was brushing his teeth he wondered, too, what had happened but his instinct was not to probe. At the moment a good night's sleep was all he asked of life and to be left alone. He had never been able to understand Anna's insatiable need to talk things over, which meant savage attacks on him and all he represented. It seemed to him simply self-indulgence, the need to get at him, to force him to respond to her, if only with anger. These scenes left him disgusted with himself and with her. Tonight he would be adamant, he thought, as he got into his pajamas.

"Sorry if I kept you waiting," he said, seeing Anna had stretched out on top of the bed and was lying there, her eyes wide open, clearly thinking or what she called thinking, which was, as far as he could see, usually on the contrary, feeling, and getting herself into a state of rage.

"You certainly take the longest time any human being ever took to brush your teeth."

"Come Fonzi, let's get some sleep," Ned said, picking the little dog up and settling him on his own blanket at the foot of the bed, before he got into bed himself and put out the light. Perhaps he could manage to be fast asleep when Anna came out of the bathroom. At least he could pretend to be.

Ned, Anna had often considered, could fall asleep by simply wishing to, as though closing a door, and she understood that falling asleep was his line of defense against her, part of the disciplined structure he imposed on himself and always had imposed no doubt, as a way of avoiding feeling anything too deeply. So when she had brushed her teeth and taken off her makeup she came back, not surprised to find him asleep.

She slipped in beside him, lay there, her arms crossed under her neck, her eyes wide open in the dark, so tense she could hardly breathe. Fonzi was snoring gently at the foot of the bed. Far down on the street a police siren screamed.

She tried to remember a time when they had been in accord, forced herself back to the days of illuminated self-discovery when her whole body had been alive down to her fingertips and the nights became brilliant journeys. It didn't matter so much then that their love-making took place in total silence on Ned's part, for she herself was such a complex of sensations, so awake and in touch with herself and with him, or so she imagined, that she took the silence as only a step in their journey together. But later when she wanted to talk, to come back to an articulate world she began to need reassurance. Had she alone experienced what she had experienced? Why couldn't Ned ever utter an endearment? After making love again and again he simply turned over and fell asleep.

He appeared to be able to separate himself from himself, to become a sexual being to the exclusion of tenderness or even love. When she felt most herself, a whole person, fulfilled in an ecstacy of sensation where the soul and the flesh seemed absolutely one, in perfect accord, he, as Ned, simply was not there. And so she began to realize after months of what appeared to be happiness that she was not there either.

"I take you in," she had whispered once, "but you never take me in."

"Didn't you come? I thought you did."

"That's not what I'm talking about."

"What are you talking about?" The note of irritability always crept in, and at first she gave up and said,

"Never mind. Go to sleep, my darling."

Then she lay awake listening to his deep breathing and wondering why she felt so lonely and even abject. So it did no good after all to try to remember . . . remembering simply brought her back into a knot of the unexpressed, the unshared, a knot of anger. Everything that Anna longed to hear, even a tone of voice, let alone loving words, she heard Ned say to Fonzi every day. Why couldn't he say such things to her? Not only that. He didn't really like her to utter her feelings towards him or even to show him, as once when after a wrangle she had taken his hand in hers and kissed it. "You're abject," Ned had said.

At the time she was still on her own wave of wanting to make peace. Only later when she remembered was she

taken by a towering rage over nothing at all, which left
Ned bewildered and furious. "I'm tired of your scenes,"
he had said. And the worst was that she understood very
well how irritating they were, and at the same time she
could never make him understand why they were, that a
storm which seemed to be about nothing at all, had been
slowly building for days.

Why did two people of such different temperaments
fall in love? Why had she married such a monster?

Anna turned over for the tenth time and tried to force
herself to relax, but if she managed to let the tension go
from her arm, it was there in her leg, then in her neck.
She looked at her watch. It was only two A.M. And suddenly she was furious with that inert sleeping man who
understood nothing and gave nothing. Unable to contain
so much fury, she took him by the throat and shook him
awake.

"For God's sake, Anna, what's the matter with you?" He
pulled her hands down and held her by the wrists and
then twisted himself into a sitting position and let her go.
"Have you gone mad?"

"No."

"It's not safe here any more."

"You are a monster," she whispered. "I just couldn't
spend another night thinking and getting nowhere . . ."

"Thinking? Thinking leads you to try to strangle me in
the middle of the night? What in hell is wrong with you,
woman?"

"I'm tired of being controlled like some biddable dog,
tired of feeling censored in everything I feel so I can
never be spontaneous, never tell you what is happening
to me, never feel free to be myself."

"Now you've upset Fonzi," Ned said vehemently. "Poor
Fonzi," for the little dog was panting and climbing all
over them in a nervous attempt to stop the loud voices.

"Poor Fonzi has been happily asleep for hours. You are
both just *beasts!*"

"Come on now," Ned was furious, "it's not Fonzi's fault. I won't take that, Anna. You had better behave." He was sheltering Fonzi under his arm now.

"What a pity that I am not a dog," Anna said.

Ned took his pillow and flung it to the floor.

"Why can't you be loving? Why? Why? Why?"

"Don't ask me to do what I can't do," Ned said coldly.

"But *why* can't you?"

This time Ned was angry enough himself to answer, "Because I don't feel like it!"

Tears poured down Anna's cheeks.

"Now we have to have the whole gambit from a violent physical attack to hysterical weeping, I suppose!"

Anna reached out to touch his hand but Ned drew it away. "Have you no pity, no compassion?" she murmured, taking a Kleenex out to blow her nose.

"What about you? You suddenly attack me at 2 A.M., for no apparent reason. Then *you* ask for pity!"

"It's hopeless," Anna said. "Put Fonzi down at the end of the bed and let's try to sleep."

"So you've had your little scene and now you can sleep . . . I can't."

And with that Ned took his pillow and left the room with Fonzi under his arm. Anna, by now in the throes of self-questioning and remorse, followed him after a few minutes with a blanket. He was stretched out on the sofa with Fonzi lying on his stomach and made no remark when she covered him, making sure Fonzi could breathe.

Then she tiptoed out into the kitchen and warmed some milk. So I've had my little scene, she said to herself and the truth was that she did feel better. The tension had been broken. It was certainly not admirable on her part but she wondered what, if anything, could break Ned open so that he would consent to talk with her. For it always ended like this, with her in tears and he in a cold withdrawal. Never, never would she know what was really happening to *him*. All she knew was his contempt and even hatred of her "moods" as he called them. He was very good at diminishing even an outbreak such as this had been into a "mood," something she herself manufactured and which had nothing whatever to do with him, was not in any way his responsibility. Possibly he did really believe he had married a mad person.

By five o'clock, as the wan light crept into the bedroom, Anna had fallen into troubled sleep, dreaming that she was lost in a strange country, following an endless path through encroaching ominous firs, without a coat and in sneakers, although there was thin snow on the ground and she was shivering with the cold. When she woke at nearly nine, Ned had left for the office. There was a note on the kitchen table, "Don't forget we are dining with Paul and Hilda."

Nothing could be worse. Paul, Ned's brother, had a sovereign talent for putting people down. He was a little mad, Anna had decided, or simply so arrogant that it became a kind of madness and it was a total mystery why Hilda, a rather good painter, had married him. They lived on the North shore in a huge nineteenth-century mansard-roofed house. Paul had a small publishing house which did special editions, a losing proposition, but distinguished in its way. "For who cares these days about fine printing?" Ned had explained, and had warned her when they were first married, "Paul will try to get at you. And the only thing is not to pay attention. Ignore him. That's the only way he can be handled."

Paul was the elder of the two brothers and it had occurred to Anna that Ned had developed his own talent for withdrawal out of self-defense. He had become a turtle to survive. But then why had he chosen to marry someone who was as open and violent as she was? What had the attraction been? He had, she sometimes thought, married a voice—for there had never been any doubt that he had fallen in love with the public person, with her power as a singer. How many times lately she had confronted him with just that. "Why do you think I can sing as I do? It's not the voice of a meek lamb, is it? What did you expect? A competent hausfrau who would never raise her voice?"

His characteristic put-down had been, "You certainly do raise it, don't you?"

Why couldn't he ever understand that the voice was the audible sign of a temperament, of someone who had, through its schooling, learned to discipline violent conflict and anxiety, that her rage was part of why she had the power she had? That she was all of a piece and could not, as he could, compartmentalize herself? Was this simply being a woman? Did women have to make themselves whole to function at all? Whereas men could afford to compartmentalize and in fact survived because they did and could? Anna was tired of the endless male-female wrangles in the press, tired of feminism, although Ned's behavior forced her into taking extreme positions in spite of herself. Nevertheless she was honest enough never to have attacked him with the trite "male chauvinist" phrase. Whatever his faults, Ned was generous where women were concerned. She had to grant that. He was naturally considerate, and from the start had helped her with housework, often cooked a meal himself, always helped her wash up. His lack of consideration had to do with his defensiveness where feelings were concerned.

The phone rang as she was having a second cup of coffee before taking Fonzi out. "Oh Mama," she breathed, "was it all right?"

But after Teresa had praised her performance and congratulated her on the warm response, Anna knew something was being withheld. "What's the matter, then? You sound strange. The *Herald?* No, I haven't seen the papers. Ned must have taken it with him." And Anna realized then that he had no doubt made off with it to spare her. "Read it to me."

There was only a short paragraph about Anna Lindstrom, and it was mostly praise, but it ended by comparing her rendition and Kathleen Ferrier's great performance of the *Lied von der Erde,* with Bruno Walter shortly before her death, and suggesting that Anna did not have the depth or the maturity for the final part. "She came close to what is needed here, but whether for technical reasons or a faulty interpretation, there seemed to be a curious lack of ease where there should have been release."

"Damn," Anna said, "Davis slowed the tempo so I had difficulty breathing . . . it wasn't fair. He had never done that in rehearsal and I was taken by surprise."

"The audience certainly did not feel as this critic did," her mother quickly comforted. "Don't pay attention, cara mia, the critic is just showing off. You know how they have to."

"It's all right, Mama. Don't try." Anna was stone cold under the blow and only wanted to get off the phone. Then she laughed, "We're going to Paul's for dinner, so it looks like a perfect day, all told." They parted on an agreement to have lunch the next day.

"Just put that review out of your mind," her mother adjured her.

"You know I can't do that. Don't ask the impossible, Mama."

Anna's first reaction had been to freeze. She did not cry, she was not angry. She had learned by now that the only way to handle a bad review was to swallow it like a glass of poison, let it work its way through her body, for the effect was at first purely physical, visceral even. And she was only too aware of what she had been up against with Kathleen Ferrier's ghost in the wings . . . She could not after all hope to match that performance with the cloud of emotion around it as everyone knew that Ferrier was dying of cancer when she sang the *Lied von der Erde* with Bruno Walter that last time!

Then she sat down in her wrapper and summoned her intelligence and her honesty. The critic had been right that something was missing in the last few minutes—and how could he have guessed what the conductor had done to her? The review must be accepted as a piece of bad luck. "It does not mean," Anna told herself, "that I cannot do it better next time."

Then on an impulse she went into the music room and took out the score, played her own accompaniment and forced herself to sing the final part as she could sing it. There alone in the apartment, she was for a half-hour so absorbed that she forgot everything in the sheer excitement and beauty she was creating for herself alone. So when the phone rang and her old friend Clara at the other end burst into a long crescendo of anger at and disappointment with the review Anna was able to say quite calmly, "A piece of bad luck, Clara—besides I really can't be expected to win over that ghost, can I? And the critic didn't know that Davis changed the tempo . . . oh well, it's all in the game, I suppose."

Clara congratulated her on her calm . . . she had no doubt expected wails and woe! But after the call Anna paced about. After all a million people were reading that she lacked maturity at this very moment! She flung on slacks and a sweater and a short coat. And Fonzi barked and barked with the joy of a walk, his tail nearly wagging itself off. Anna picked him up, kissed him, and off they went. Of course, she met a neighbor in the elevator who insisted on talking about the review, and that did not help at all, although he had been at the concert and was reassuring.

"You got an ovation," he said. "I wouldn't let the *Herald* spoil that for a moment."

"The trouble is he was right," Anna said and regretted it immediately. Why expose herself further, even to admitting her own failing? Ned would never do that himself or condone it. He had never in the two years since their marriage admitted that he could be wrong. And now here she was adding fuel to the fire.

"Well, I'm sorry you feel that—don't let them get you down."

One thing Anna hated about the apartment was that it was impossible to taste the air. Now outdoors on Beacon Street she was met by wonderfully crisp invigorating October weather. Fonzi trotted along beside her. It felt good to be out, anonymous, alone with the companionable little dog. Anna took deep breaths and made a try at shutting out all that was troubling her that morning, but when she sat down on a bench near the pond in the Public Gardens to rest for a moment there was no shutting disaster out. She was helpless against the tide of depression—her violence of the night, the unexpected attack on her professional self, Ned's characteristic leaving without saying goodbye.

"Oh Fonzi," she said, stroking Fonzi's silky ears and letting him lick her hand, "it's an awfully lonely business." Lonely to be married to Ned, but what she could not ever explain even to Teresa, lonely to be in that ceaseless battle to develop and refine a talent, lonely to appear on a stage before a thousand people and summon what it takes to give a good performance. The endless anxiety, the endless pressure, and the almost certain disappointments along the way. One of Anna's fantasies had always been to give it all up, live as ordinary people did—but then, did they? Was there such a thing as an "ordinary life"? When Anna looked around her it seemed that everyone she knew was engaged in some impossible battle . . . Clara with her alcoholic husband, Mary with apparently no way to get published after all these years of sending poems out . . . and she had genius, Anna was convinced. No, Anna, she admonished herself. You simply cannot complain.

"Come on, Fonzi, we are going to prove that we can be tough!"

Chapter II

When he got home at half-past five, Ned was astonished to find Anna apparently perfectly calm. For a moment he wondered whether she had not seen the paper, but then he noticed the *Herald* on the coffee table, folded at the review, and decided at once to say nothing about it.

"They expect us at seven. I guess I have time for a cup of tea before I shower."

"I'll get it for you."

While Anna was in the kitchen, Ned talked to Fonzi and then rubbed his eyes, rubbing the long tiresome day out of them. After that he looked around and decided to lie down on the floor and try to get the kinks out of his back, but a person who chose to lie on the floor was fair game and Fonzi leapt upon him barking excitedly, licking his face, coming back for more when pushed away. It was hopeless and Ned was laughing and thoroughly rumpled when Anna brought him a cup of tea and a piece of cinnamon toast.

"Thanks," he said. "That looks good."

And after Anna had sat down on the edge of a chair he handed her *The Evening Globe*. "You'd better look at the review," he said, "It's quite a good one."

"I didn't dare buy it—after the *Herald*," she said, ruffling it through to find the page, then reading with great concentration.

This time there were no odious comparisons but instead the reviewer remarked on her "delicacy of tone, and perfect command of the music. Anna Lindstrom has the voice for Mahler. She can handle the transitions as few of her contemporaries can. A well-tempered instrument. The ovation at the end was deserved."

Ned was waiting for Anna to say something. She didn't. After reading the review she folded the paper and laid it on the table.

"I'll just go and change while you finish your tea." But as she went by his chair, she kissed the top of his head. So, Ned thought, maybe after all she was not going to behave like a wounded tigress. He had dreaded coming home not knowing what he would find: Anna in bed ill and refusing to go out to dinner, Anna weeping and pacing the floor, Anna in a state of silent gloom. Instead he had found a docile wife who made him a cup of tea! Well, you never knew.

"It's going to be all right, Fonzi," he said, stroking Fonzi's ears and submitting to being thoroughly licked before he went back to *The New Yorker*. All right as far as last night's performance went . . . but that was only one layer of their life together. And the more intimate side of it was not getting any better, as far as he could see or know. Ned had convinced himself that the only way to understand Anna was to consider her a Jekyll and Hyde. The insoluable problem for him was that he could never tell which side was operating at any given moment nor when to make his escape. A scene like that of last night left him closed in on himself, cold as ice. He appeared to have married a woman whom he admired as an artist, who could still trouble and even transport him when she sang, but whom he could not admire as a woman, whom he was beginning to find tiresome, for whom he sometimes felt contempt. Lack of control, irrational anger, as he called it, was high on his list of severe flaws. He had even gone so far one afternoon on his weekly call at his mother's to ask her whether she and his father had ever engaged in violent scenes of anger.

"Anger?" she had said, raising an eyebrow, "What a thing to imagine!"

"You were never cross with him?"

"If I was, I didn't show it," she said, and as he waited in silence, she built her defenses, "Of course, Ned, times have changed. When I was married the unbuttoned behavior of today would have been impossible—that was for the immigrants, not for us. But why are you asking me such a question?"

"Anna is very cross with me," Ned said. "Almost everything about me seems an irritation." Even as he said it he regretted it.

"You have to remember that Anna is not one of us," his mother said, pouring herself another cup of tea and swallowing it with so much relish, it was clear at once that his confession was not unwelcome.

"She is immensely gifted, so, you are right, she is not one of us!" he said firmly. "We are ordinary people. She is not."

"She is half Italian, after all."

"She is also half Swedish. Why is it better to be half Swedish than half Italian? Why do you imply that the latter is somehow not quite acceptable?"

"I didn't imply that at all. All I meant was that the Italians are temperamentally rather unlike us."

"Anna is unlike me, that's for sure," Ned said stiffly, "But I would myself shy away from generalities, especially in regard to a towering personality such as hers!"

"I'm sorry you are not getting on," his mother said gently. "Would it help if I had a little talk with her? I do after all know you somewhat better than she does and have known you for forty years!"

Ned swallowed the word, "You haven't any idea what I'm really like," and murmured something about perhaps not betraying his confidence.

"I wanted you to be happy," his mother said then in a querulous voice he knew only too well, the voice that always put him in the wrong somehow.

"I didn't marry for happiness," Ned said.

"What did you marry for, then? What a strange thing to say."

"I married because I was enormously interested. Until Anna, women had not interested me very much, I'm afraid."

Ned was still entangled in remembering that talk with his mother when Anna came back, dressed, he realized, in that dark blue dress with a flaring collar which she had worn when he proposed marriage. Was it an apology?

"Wow!" he said, getting up, "You're looking very grand."

"I always feel I have to be in armor to meet Paul. This dress is my armor."

"Is it indeed?" Ned teased. "You were not inclined to be a fortress the night I proposed marriage, if I remember."

"Darling, I couldn't be a fortress against you."

It was easy to kiss her then. And as he did Ned felt stirred as he had not been for weeks.

"Why do we do such awful things to each other?" she said, running a finger along his mouth.

Ned restrained the impulse to argue that *he* had done nothing "awful" and went in to have a shower. And Anna went into the music room and took the Duparc songs out. She was just finishing one of Ned's favorites, *"Mon enfant, ma soeur, songe à la douceur, d'aller là-bas vivre ensemble,"* when he stood in the doorway, dressed and ready to go. She was not aware of his presence, at least did not acknowledge it, and Ned for a few moments soared with her on that remarkable voice. It flowed over him like a pardon, like a justification. He couldn't utter a word. And when she turned to him with one of her deep looks, all he could say was, "I'll get your coat."

"Damn Paul! I wish you were taking me out to dinner."

The Paul Fraser's house had always both charmed and intimidated Anna. The high-ceilinged rooms and long French windows were spacious enough to contain a vast clutter of objets d'art, books, and paintings, without seeming crowded, and she had learned to let Paul achieve pinnacles of rudeness on their arrival because that was the way he apparently had to operate: first knock your guests over the head, silence them, and then talk without stopping for at least a half-hour.

So she took it calmly when she uttered her pleasure at going into the library where books were piled on every end table and chair, and Paul's answer was "I should think it would be a pleasant change from that morgue you and Ned have chosen to live in."

Instead of reacting as Paul perhaps hoped she would, for he liked to draw blood, Anna suddenly chuckled, then laughed.

"What's so funny about that? I can't understand anyone choosing to live in an apartment and then to make it look like a page from *House Beautiful!*"

Ned had disappeared into the kitchen with Hilda and for a second Anna felt panic, but she was still laughing. "You are so preposterous, Paul. If someone put you into a novel, no one would believe it."

"Several people have, as a matter of fact."

She moved closer to the fire for the house was chilly,

and on this October evening one window was open, but she did not sit down. "Good novels?"

"Of course not. There are no Prousts around these days."

Was he laughing at himself? One of the fascinating things about Paul had always been whether he was serious or his arrogance only an affectation, armor against the world which must judge him as not a success, at least in relation to his powerful younger brother.

Ned and Hilda came in then, Ned carrying a tray of champagne glasses and Hilda, the bottle in a silver container of ice.

"We were talking about Paul as the subject of a novel," Anna said demurely.

"The hero of this imaginary novel had better open the champagne," Hilda said. Anna had observed that she treated her husband rather as one might treat a spoiled child, nearly always managing to be amused rather than offended by his behavior.

"Champagne, eh? And what is the occasion for such a splurge?"

"We have with us this evening, a diva, and a toast in champagne is in order, I felt." Hilda sounded firm.

"You know I prefer Scotch," he said, taking the bottle out and skillfully loosening the wire fastening.

"Yes, but tonight you are being deprived . . ."

"I'm sorry, Paul, it's my fault! Can't he have Scotch?" Anna was smiling and as she caught Ned's eye began to laugh again.

"That's right—laugh at him! He's quite impossible!"

The cork flew out and Paul poured the champagne. "I presume there's another bottle? This won't take us very far."

Paul was sitting and had already taken a swallow, so Hilda and Ned stood alone and Ned lifted his glass, and proposed a toast, "To Anna Lindstrom who has given us much joy!"

"Now can I sit down comfortably and drink?" Anna asked. Ned was being very kind and she was touched. In fact she felt tears in her eyes.

"You're not going to cry, are you?" Paul asked. "The diva is not going to give us a scene?"

"Oh, I could at the drop of a hat!"

"Or a name? Kathleen Ferrier, for instance," Paul needled.

"No fair!" Hilda said.

"When has Paul ever been fair?" Ned said lightly, but Anna knew he was cross. His face was quite red.

"I heard you were marvelous," Hilda interposed quickly.

"Only not quite as marvelous as Kathleen Ferrier," Anna said quietly. This time she was not going to rise to any provocation.

"We heard her in London, didn't we, Hilda?" Paul said happily. "She was absolutely smashing in something or other . . ."

"*Orpheus and Eurydice,*" Hilda said. "She was very ill then, and everyone knew it."

"All I need is cancer," Anna said, but regretted it at once, and looked across at Ned in shame. That was the trouble. However hard she tried to keep the balance Paul always managed to make her teeter at some moment. But she recovered. "I never had the luck to hear her, but I have studied the records. She was beyond compare. And I would like to propose a toast to her!"

"Bravo!" Ned said, lifting his glass.

"And now shall we change the subject?" Paul asked irritably.

"By all means. Whose feathers shall we ruffle next?" Ned asked, smiling across at Anna. "What's in the works, Paul? What new poet have you discovered?"

"Poet? Nonsense, there aren't any poets. It's the age of infamy, self-advertisement. The confessional has ceased to be a box with a priest and a sinner in it, and is now the

entire reading public and some people who can't read—
and an exhibitionist who can't write. Poets?" He laughed
scornfully.

"So whom are you publishing?"

"An exegesis of Wallace Stevens."

"Old hat, old boy," Ned said. "Surely that's been done
into the ground."

"I must go and finish cooking our dinner," Hilda announced.

"I'll come with you," Anna said quickly, delighted for
the chance to escape and also for the chance to talk with
Hilda. "I can mix the salad or make myself useful in some
way, I trust." They took their glasses and left.

"Make yourself comfortable," Hilda said. "There really
isn't much you can do. But I wanted to have you for myself
for a little while. Paul is so impossible."

Anna sat on a high stool and looked around. "I love your
kitchen," she said. There were pots of herbs on the window sill, a long shelf of cookbooks, the kind of disorder
that has meaning . . . pots and pans hanging from the
ceiling, everything close at hand that could be needed.
But also in a remarkably large space. The windows looked
out on a vegetable garden inside a high wall, "Sometimes
I envy your life here . . ."

"Good heavens, why? Now the children are all away at
school or college it's much too big for us, really."

"Paul is right, you know. Our apartment is cold. And I
guess that is because neither of us wanted to impose our
past, so we ended up with a kind of blank good taste. I
really like the Beverly house much better, but we only
manage a rare weekend there these days. I'm away an
awful lot, Ned too, with all those meetings. I don't think
we've started to live our real life yet. Do you suppose we
ever will?

Hilda came over and gave Anna a hug, "I love you,
Anna, you're so open."

"Ned hates that."

"I expect he does. All the Frasers are knotted up so tight, so afraid. Paul buries himself under mountains of antagonism because he is so afraid of being found out."

Why had she married Paul? Anna had longed to ask the question for two years, but she still didn't quite dare.

"Does he mind your painting?"

"Oh, I expect so," Hilda said, putting the salad together, her back to Anna now. "We never talk about it. He isn't interested . . . and maybe that's just as well!"

"Are you working now?"

"Yes. Isn't it wonderful?—I'm in a great burst of painting. I'm breaking out of the abstract at last. I'm going crazy over flowers. Born again, I feel!"

"Ah . . . it must be marvelous to be able to do what you want to do, not to have to wait to be asked, not to have to finagle and wait and hope for a chance. I'd give my eye teeth to sing Orpheus!"

"Ned is supportive, isn't he? That must be a great help."

"Yes," Anna left it at that. "Do you and Paul ever fight?"

"We used to."

"How did you make your peace?"

"We didn't. We gave up trying to change each other."

"Oh."

"Hey, we'd better get out the champagne . . . dinner is just about ready."

Anna hated to leave the kitchen and Hilda. There were so many things their brief exchange had started in her mind. Was every marriage a battle for emotional territory, for instance? Was the antagonism part of violent attachment, the thing that aroused anger and even hatred . . . because . . . because . . . But they had, of course, to go back into the lion's den. Obediently she went back into the library, bearing the champagne. The cold air hit her, an icy blast from the open window.

"You must be an Eskimo, Paul," she said, shivering.

"Well, we can close the window," Ned got up and closed it.

"Not an Eskimo," Paul said irritably, "we are Anglo-Saxons. Don't you know how they always have the windows wide open in England?"

"Yes, and have chilblains," Ned said.

"Hilda and I never have colds," he said, apparently affronted.

"Neither does Anna. She can't afford to catch cold, she must be protected."

"So fragile," Paul murmured as his wife came in to join them. "You open this one, Ned, I've lost my grip."

And while Ned struggled, Paul got up and put a big log on the fire. It was a concession, as Anna gratefully realized.

"One glass and we'll be on our way into the dining room," Hilda said. "I hope you're hungry, fragile or not."

"Of course," Anna said, "I'm as strong as an ox!"

"Good at hauling logs?" Paul gave his short laugh rather like a bark.

"Good at singing," Ned said. "It takes a lot of strength to produce that amazing sound out of your throat!"

"But what must make you feel fragile is that you are your own instrument. It must be scary," Hilda said. "Do you wake up on the morning of a concert wondering if you have a voice?"

"Oh, she is silent as the grave," Ned smiled, "can't get a word out of her. And it's best to keep away, as I have learned."

"I'm really a monster," Anna announced, "not fit for human consumption."

"A *monstre sacré* then," Paul mused. "I've always believed it is a mistake to want to know a performer. Distance makes the magic, or would you disagree, old Ned?"

"Sometimes I would agree," Ned said, smiling at Anna. She knew he was only teasing.

"You have a very good effect on Ned," Anna said, lifting her glass."

"He's a brave man. He married the magic."

"I married a woman, not a piece of magic," Ned said.

"Thank goodness," Anna was laughing, "I have wondered . . ."

"What were you talking about?" Hilda asked then. "I could hear laughter."

"Oh, we were reminiscing. Paul says I treated him very badly when we were kids. He had an awful temper, you know. I used to tease him on purpose to make him flare up. But I taught him to sail . . . you have to admit that was kind of me, Paul."

"You needed a slave on that boat of yours."

"Come," Hilda said, "we really must eat or the roast will be overdone."

But somehow the atmosphere had warmed and the rest of the evening was comparatively painless, especially since they found themselves in total agreement about the incredible new Secretary of the Interior and for once Paul's negative comments seemed appropriate. Anna enjoyed the discussion, enjoyed not talking or thinking about music, enjoyed seeing Ned show passionate commitment. This he could do, she was aware, because forests, the water level in the Southwest, the dangers of oil drilling offshore could be approached intellectually.

Besides, tonight she sensed that they were emerging from battle into some kind of peace, however temporary. On the drive back to town, they talked for once. Anna was on a high beam of pleasure and relief that she had taken Paul's insults without reacting. For once she was not in the wrong. For once Paul had not succeeded in making her feel inferior, as they so often did without even knowing what they were doing, members of a secret society to which she could never belong, however well she behaved.

"Why is Paul such a rude man?" she asked. "What makes him tick?"

"I don't know . . ."

"You must have some idea . . . after all you grew up together. I was fascinated that he let you teach him to sail, it seemed unlike him, somehow. And you were younger."

"As a matter of fact he was emerging from a kind of breakdown after our father died. It was the psychiatrist's idea that he needed something physical to do, something to take his mind off himself." Ned absent-mindedly took her hand in his right one. "Do we have to talk about Paul?"

"No."

There was a silence then. Anna leaned her head on the seat back.

"You were marvelous, Anna, I must say."

"It isn't worth the battle with him . . . just a waste of energy and emotion."

"Well!" Ned squeezed her hand and let it go, as he was passing a truck. "Since when have you been afraid to waste emotion?"

"I don't waste it on people I don't love, Ned," she said quietly. But for once she did not want to pursue what could end in pain. And it was she this time who changed the subject.

"It must be hell to be married to him," she said.

"In a way, you know, I think Paul was relieved to be with me on the boat and not to have to make any decisions."

"He seems so decisive, so sure he is right. Are you suggesting that Hilda captains their boat?"

"I wasn't thinking about that. Paul and I fought a lot always . . . you see, he was older than I, but I was brighter, and he was in a perpetual state of fury because I could do most things better than he could. Except write or say things in words . . . he was always very good at that."

"And you, my preposterous darling, were very bad at that."

"Yes, I was. Words seemed always disorderly to me, not to be trusted . . . not like a mathematical equation where you had the answer or you didn't. On the boat I had the right answers and Paul had to accept that I did."

"But didn't he mind being ordered about?"

"Well," Ned paused for a few seconds, "I suppose he did. But he had been ill, really suicidal . . . I guess he needed something quite simple like being a sailor. It was a kind of pact between us, not to fight on the boat. So it was restful."

"What did your father's death do to you?"

"Locked me in. We became the prisoners of mother's grief. And her grief was so awful that we were made to feel we had no right to ours. She never admitted it, but she was furious with Paul for trying to commit suicide. And she never forgave him. For years I was the buffer between them. Between her silent disapproval and his outbursts of anger. By the time he was twenty Paul hated everybody, you see."

"Poor Paul. And poor you."

"Then much to everyone's amazement Paul married— am I boring you?" Ned asked suddenly.

"Of course not. At last we are talking about something important, don't you see?"

"You didn't know you were marrying into such a family of eccentrics, did you? Why did you marry me anyway?"

"Because I liked your nose."

"Not likely."

"Likely." After a moment's pause Anna began to think out loud. It was something that could be done when they were sitting side by side in the car, she had discovered. It permitted silences without tension. Then they were not facing each other, but looking out at the world moving past, the lights, a man on a bicycle, a truck to be passed. Thinking aloud, she said, "I felt we were equals. You see, often the people who fell in love with me were somehow not my equals . . . that sounds arrogant. But I have achieved something and it frightens people. Everyone told me how powerful you are in your world . . . and that was reassuring. But now I have the feeling that in your mind there is no equality. You make me feel inferior. It's like living with a governess. I can never be myself with you."

"What I don't understand is why being a screaming hysteric is 'being yourself'. I am alienated by your tantrums. I can't help it."

"I feel like a tigress in too small a cage, can't you see?" But even as she said this Anna knew it was hopeless, and as always, a little beside the point, an evasion on her part, because she had not come to terms with her anger, herself. And it caused her acute shame. And as Ned made no answer she leaned for a moment against his shoulder.

"I think you were conditioned never to allow yourself anger. Was it considered a crime in your mother's house?"

"Yes, it was."

"Why?"

"We were brought up to believe that the surfaces must be kept pleasant."

"And if they were, then everything was presumed to be all right? So your brother tried to commit suicide and you bury your feelings so deep you can't behave like a human being!"

"It's a matter of ethos, Anna, can't you see?"

"Oh yes, I see all right," Anna said bitterly. "But you married someone with quite a different ethos."

"Unbuttoned ego, my mother calls it."

"I think it's much healthier to let anger out than to bury it so deep you don't even know it is there."

"It may be better for oneself but it's hard on other people."

"Oh Ned, do you think it's easy on me when you freeze up against me? Can't you see that that is just as punishing as you feel I am when I attack you? And it's worse, maybe, because you refuse to have it out. You refuse to talk. And every time you do that and bury your own anger, we get further apart."

"Yes, we do," Ned said stiffly.

The moment when the door might have opened had closed again, Anna knew.

"Maybe we'll have good weather on the weekend."

"I hope so . . . it's the last chance to get bulbs in . . . I'll be in Pittsburgh the following weekend, you know."

"Well, let's try to have a calm country time," Ned said. "I could do with a little peace."

Anna refrained from answering that. All it needs for peace is for you to give a little, be a little loving for a change. She did not say it. A tiny triumph of will over impulse. When she censored herself in this way she won. But what did she win? she asked herself. A small respite in a war that would not change, and at a high cost. For every time she buried her impulse the seed of resentment got planted.

There was no love-making that night. Fonzi slept between them.

Chapter III

Anna had often asked herself why she felt so comfortable in the cottage, and she always had from their first weekend there together. It had no view of the ocean and had become over the years a repository for odds and ends of furniture, some wicker-arm chairs and a chaise lounge on the screened-in porch, a mixture of modern Danish and early American set incongruously on a blue Chinese rug in the rather small living room. But all this and even the Sargent water colors discarded from the big house, gave it an atmosphere at once casual and lively. It had what Anna had always longed for, the air of places much lived in by a single family, "background" was the word that sprang to mind. At any rate she felt at ease in it and had from the beginning. The happiest times she and Ned shared had always been here.

Ned had no need to analyze it, it was simply home to him, full of childhood memories, for when they were in college Paul and he had shared it for several summers of sailing and playing tennis and giving small house parties.

But the chief thing for both Anna and Ned was that here they could each shed their public personalities, wear old blue jeans, and above all work outdoors.

And on this October morning they were hard at it, planting tulips, while Fonzi barked at squirrels, then unburied an old bone which he was now happily chewing under a bush. It had come as a surprise to Anna that one of Ned's passions was gardening. It was he who had staked out quite a large garden at the back of the house and had it walled-in with brick like an English garden, cutting trees ruthlessly to do it. But all that was before Anna. And it had been for him a new pleasure to work with her. It was not a thing he had imagined when he proposed marriage.

"Hey, we forgot the bone meal," he called out from his end of the border they were planting.

"There must be some in the garage," she answered, "I'll go see."

It always amused Ned to see Anna in her work clothes and he watched her walk away with a twinkle in his eye. The statuesque Anna of the concert stage metamorphosed into a rather stout boy, her surprisingly plump legs shown off to great effect today by her short shorts. She's a damned attractive woman, he was thinking, as he carefully dug a circle of holes with neat quick expertise.

"I found it," she called and laid the bag of bone meal at his feet.

"You do it so well," she said, watching him pour a little bone meal in each hole, then set the tulips in. He didn't stop but talked for a moment as he filled in the holes and patted the earth hard around each.

"I learned from my Uncle Henry, that silent man. I learned from watching him—and from being solemnly told off by him, too. I can still hear him saying 'gardening does not take much intelligence, but it does take a little. You are planting those anemones upside down.'"

"Oh dear," Anna was laughing, "how awful! What did you do then?"

"Dug them up and started again."

Anna went off, still amused, to go on setting in a square of *iris reticulata*. But Ned's story stuck in her mind as she turned one wrinkled flat bulb in her hand and could not decide which was right side up. "A little intelligence is necessary," she reminded herself, glancing over at the totally absorbed Ned. What if?

"You're having trouble, old girl."

"How did you know?"

"Oh, that rather ominous silence, I expect. Look for a tiny thread—that would be a root—that will tell you which side up."

"But sometimes there is no tiny thread to be seen," she protested.

"In that case, say a short prayer."

Anna was kneeling, and before she had finished, her knees as well as her hands and face, were black. "I might as well be making mud pies," she said, "and I can hardly move I'm so stiff.

Ned stood up then, his hands on his hips to stretch his back, took one look at her and burst out laughing.

"I know," she said, laughing too, "it's not fair. You dig and dig and look perfectly clean after hours of it!"

"I wish your ardent public could see you now!"

"They would get a shock, wouldn't they? Oh Ned, I'm out of breath."

He looked at his watch, "Well, in a half-hour we'll take a break. Did you put the beer in the fridge?"

"Natch."

"We've got to get fifty in today, come hell or high water."

"Well, what next?"

Next was a bag of peony tulips to be set in behind the iris and Ned suggested a few here and there in between them. Anna whistled an aria from Carmen while she worked. Why couldn't it always be like this? Companionable. Silent. Happy.

Now they were working side by side, but the trouble was that their real lives were so far apart there seemed to be no communication possible any longer. This was not their real life, after all, it was Marie Antoinette's imitation farm where she and her ladies could disport themselves and pretend to be peasants, could get their hands dirty and play at planting potatoes.

"Why isn't this real?" she asked aloud.

"It is."

"Is it?" Anna stood up and stretched, "Ned, I'm exhausted. I've got to stop."

"Just let me finish—just ten more and this lot will be in the ground."

"I'm going in."

Anna had learned not to go beyond a certain point in fatigue. She would need exceptional physical as well as psychic energy in the week ahead, to get ready for the *B-Minor Mass* in Pittsburgh. And as she showered and washed the earth from her hands and face and arms and legs she already felt the change in her, the change toward a performance that would demand all she had to give. Already she could feel her nerves tensing up, a little like an athlete getting ready for a race, that summoning of all her powers to a single end. She was shivering as she dried herself off, for exactly as though a cloud had moved across the sun, the poison of that review was moving across her, a dark shadow she had to contain, and push aside a thousand times, surmount.

When Ned came in, cheerful and relaxed, she had sandwiches ready and glasses on a tray. But she felt unrelated, out of touch.

"I'm hungry," he announced, "I think I'll just wash my hands and shower later." And in a few minutes he was sitting beside her, where she had stretched out on the chaise lounge.

"The leaves are falling—look Ned, they are like thin gold pieces falling."

"Mmmm," he said, munching his sandwich. "It's been too dry, an early fall, it looks like." For a moment they ate in silence.

"That's a hell of a good sandwich, Anna."

"I'm glad you approve."

"But you've hardly touched yours."

"Not hungry," she said, taking a sip of beer.

"You worked too hard," he sounded quite solicitous.

"I can't keep up with you, my friend, but I enjoyed myself. I felt like a good animal."

"Whatever do you mean by that?"

"Oh I don't know, physically alive, comfortable in my body . . . you know, Ned. Surely you know."

"Well, yes. I feel good, if that's what you mean," and he added, "Do we have to analyze it?"

"No. Do you want some apple pie? Coffee?"

"I'll get it. You stay here and rest."

On the surface he could be so gentle and polite, and that's what he wanted, a smooth untroubled, untroubling surface. He wanted to enjoy life without trying to probe. "Why analyze it?" Anna asked herself. Because for me living is finding out what is really happening to me, and that's the last thing Ned wants. He could never admit the shadow. It was too frightening, perhaps. He too in his way was like an athlete, one for whom everything could be measured in terms of achievement. So even love-making was a matter simply of orgasm, a purely physical release. As often happened when Anna had made a physical effort, the release for her, came with a rush of feelings and thoughts. He rested by not being. She rested by being.

Anna had gone for a little walk around the garden, picked a small bunch of dahlias and chrysanthemums, crimson and orange, a dissonance that pleased her, when Ned came out to the porch with a tray.

"Hey," Ned said, "I call that a riot of color."

"I like it," Anna said, prickling as she always did when Ned punctured her balloons with irony.

"I would add a touch of white . . . there's that achillea somewhere."

"No," Anna said, "The whole point is that clash of primary color—not that it matters," she added.

"But it does seem to matter," Ned said, suddenly irritated himself. Anna couldn't take the slightest criticism, he was thinking, even about a bunch of flowers. And he was damned if he was to be a sycophant like most of her friends. "Come on, let's eat our pie while it's hot."

"I suppose people could go to war about a matter of taste," Anna said, trying to get away from her own irritation, and accepting her plate and a fork.

"No doubt about it. If I had known you would put crimson and orange together, I would never have married you," he teased.

"That's almost too true," Anna said, thinking of the hundred ways in which she irritated Ned these days, so no subject, not even a bunch of flowers was safe any longer. Leaving her pie half-eaten, she went in to find a vase . . . " or they will die, poor things, while we are discussing them."

She had trouble finding the right one—Ned had such definite ideas about things in this house. But finally she decided on a small Venetian glass flecked with gold.

"There," she said, setting it down beside Ned, "How is that?"

Then she saw that Ned had not been able to resist changing her bunch, had picked a spray of white anemone while she was making up her mind. Now he placed it deftly in the center of the Venetian glass, with her flowers.

"Perfect," he announced. "I bought that vase in Venice, I've always liked it."

And Anna, eager to make peace, said, "Let's take it home with us." For she knew it was quite absurd to let a little thing like this bunch of flowers create tension between them.

"If you wish," Ned said, and it was clear that he himself did *not* wish. "Finish your pie, Anna."

"Do you think the apartment is the trouble?" she asked

for she realized that she had herself hesitated as she used the word "home."

"Whatever are you getting at now?" Ned asked. "Can't we even disagree about a bunch of flowers without its becoming an issue between us?"

But Anna couldn't stop now. "The apartment doesn't feel like home. It has become the place where we don't meet, the place where we wrangle and sleep. That's what I meant. You have to admit that you did hesitate when I suggested we take your precious Venetian glass there, didn't you?"

"Oh, come, Anna, you are making a mountain out of a molehill!" He would never admit it to Anna but with her x-ray mind for sensing things, she had sensed that he did not want to take the vase to the apartment. He sometimes felt that he could not stand being pin-pointed like this another day. It was like living with some sort of witch. "Can't we have a little peace, even here?"

"Only on the surface," Anna said.

"Well, for God's sake, let's settle for the surface then."

"Very well, you beast, you prehistoric animal, lumbering off for cover at the slightest whisper from a human being!"

"We are not going to have a scene, Anna, and spoil this day." And once more she was being put down like an importunate child. How well she knew Ned's look, his mouth in a thin closed line, his whole face closed against her.

"You never give me credit for anything," she said. "I didn't turn a hair when Paul insulted me and tried to get a rise out of me the other night. I behaved very well."

"Yes, you did. For once. And now I suppose you have to make up for it by attacking me."

Whatever happened it always had to be her fault. And perhaps, after all, it was her fault. That was what made Anna feel like a cripple or a mad person most of the time.

It was she, true enough, who "made the scenes."

"You talk about love," Ned said, taking a cigar out of the box on the table and lighting it carefully, "but all I see is hatred and violence."

"And all you give me is coldness and withdrawal when I try to reach you, try to make you understand. If only you would listen, once, Ned, really listen, not rush to close the door on me whenever I try to talk honestly with you!"

"Am I allowed to smoke out here on the porch?" he asked with cold courtesy.

"Yes, if you blow the smoke out of my way. Oh Ned, what is the matter with us?" It was an attempt to break the spiral of anger which over and over again in the past year wound itself tighter and tighter but it was too late. "Do you think I enjoy being angry? Do you think it's a pleasure?"

"I sometimes think you are an addict—as some people take to the bottle, you take to anger."

"But why should I?"

"From what you tell me you have always been an angry person. You had tantrums as a child. How many times you come back from a concert furious at someone or something! I suppose it breaks all that tension you talk about, but it never occurs to you apparently, that other people bear the brunt of it. You may feel better as a result but I feel real resentment at being your whipping boy."

"Yes," Anna said, "I know you do." Then she added half to herself, "It's like a maze. You can't break your way out of a maze . . . you have to discover the pattern, find your way through . . . only I don't know how to do that. Does anyone ever criticize you, Ned? Are you so powerful at the bank that you are above criticism? Has it never occurred to you that you are not always right? And that other people are not always wrong?"

"There's no point in this," Ned said icily. "We aren't getting anywhere."

"I wish I knew how you regard me, what you really think I am."

"Do you really want to know?" He was looking straight at her, but with a look so cold, of such distaste that Anna hesitated, but after all she had to say "yes."

Ned took a puff of his cigar. "I think you are two people, Jekyll and Hyde. One is a great personality, a lovable, beautiful woman, with a touch of genius."

"And the other?"

"The other is a screaming peacock—you call me arrogant!—a wilful witch who cannot be criticized without an outburst, totally self-indulgent. You asked for it," he added. He might as well have slapped her hard on the face. And for a long moment Anna was silent, while her heart thumped like an animal inside her.

"I'm whole," she said then, "I cannot compartmentalize myself. I'm not two people, one good and beautiful, the other bad and ugly. I'm one whole person, Ned." Where was the clue to this dreadful maze? How would they ever find the way out? "You have to take the whole person."

"I can't do that. I do not find what you call the whole person acceptable."

"You ask me to censor myself all the time—I am becoming the prisoner of your ethos, and it is making me ill. I have an awfully scary performance ahead. How can I sing when I have to censor myself all the time?" The words tumbled out.

"Well, concentrate on your performance then and leave me out of it, leave the prehistoric animal out of it!"

"Oh Ned, I can't. I can't compartmentalize as you can. You can apparently go off to the office perfectly calm and do your work after one of these awful fights. I feel it in my throat, in my voice itself, like a dreadful crack. Can't you see?" She was crying now and got up, rushed out to the kitchen to find a Kleenex and try to pull herself together.

When she came back she asked through her tears, hating the tears, the weakness of it. "Have you never cried, Ned?"

"No."

"Not when your father died?"

"No. I hated my mother's endless tears too much. I hate your tears."

"You have made that abundantly clear."

"Where's Fonzi?" Ned asked, suddenly aware that though Fonzi had been with them in the garden, he had not been seen for an hour. He ran out into the garden calling, "Come dog! Fonzi, come!"

There was total silence. Then after what seemed an eternity they heard a short bark from somewhere in the bushes behind the house.

"It's all right," Ned called back. Fonzi, it appeared, had found a chipmunk hole and had been digging furiously and made himself absolutely filthy. Even his ears were covered with dirt and his nose was black. Ned carried him into the house. Anna followed.

"We'll just put him in the tub," she said, "right now," and she turned the water on while Ned held him.

"It's lucky I didn't shower . . . I'm filthy, too."

Fonzi couldn't lead them out of the maze, Anna was thinking, as she lathered him with a cake of soap, but he could give them a respite.

And Ned said, "You gave us an awful scare, Fonzi. What if you had been run over, you dirty little dog?"

Chapter IV

Going home in the car they were silent, Fonzi lying between them. Ned had turned the car radio on and they
listened to a Beethoven sonata. Every now and then Anna
stroked Fonzi's ears, still a little damp after his bath.

Ned was thinking that it would be a relief to have Anna
away for a few days. Maybe he could get back to normal,
sort things out, cease to feel every hair on his head prickle
with irritation. The day had started out so well, why had
she spoiled it? Over nothing. A bunch of flowers. There
had been laughter over that at first, and then it all turned
to rage. What in hell have I done to be the target of so
much anger? Watching her walk across the lawn in her
shorts he had felt a moment of desire, then of course it all
got mixed up, blotted out, and all he could feel was a wish
to be left alone, not to have to cope with this irrational
woman whom he had once thought he loved, whom he
had taken into his life, taken into himself . . . it was like
going to bed with a bunch of nettles, he thought.

"What are you thinking?" she finally asked on the out-
skirts of Boston as the traffic began to slow them down.

"I was thinking that a few days of peace without you are
going to be highly desirable."

"Yes," she said. "I know."

For now as usual Anna was filled with remorse and

anxiety. Always after these fights she struggled with herself, to get under the anger to what was really happening and to face the dragon in its lair. Something had to change. But she was too realistic to imagine that she could change radically . . . people don't change, she knew. Hilda had talked about accepting Paul, about their accepting each other. So they had managed to stay together. But at what cost? Still, Hilda was painting and painting well. Had she done that by shutting Paul out? By living along beside him without asking or expecting communion and understanding? How far could she, Anna, compromise, for peace? A marriage then became like a burnt-out house in which two people managed to exist among the ruins. How could she sing, stifled and censored? Ned had suggested that she leave him out of it and concentrate on music. Very well, Anna thought, that is what I shall do.

But it was easier to think about this than to bring it to pass, she discovered the next morning when she was going over the score with her teacher, Mariana Protopova, an old Russian woman who had worked with Anna for the past two years.

"Your voice is not clear," Protopova said after they had worked for a half-hour, going over one section a half-dozen times. "And besides, you are not breathing quite easily, are you? Whatever have you been doing, Anna? The sound is blurred."

"I know," Anna said, pushing her hair back. "I don't feel well."

"But the concert is on Saturday!" Protopova was not easy on her pupils. For her the music was what mattered and she was visibly irritated if not actually hurt when Bach was ill-served, especially by Anna Lindstrom. "Come, take a deep breath. We'll start again. Concentrate, Anna!"

But Anna was now paralyzed by fear. The concert was on Saturday. She could never do it. Protopova was bent over the piano entirely concentrating herself on the accompaniment, singing in a hoarse voice, apparently unaware that, far from taking a deep breath, Anna was standing there, numb, unable to make a sound.

"You've missed the entrance, donkey!"

"I can't do it," Anna said. "That review eats into me like a poison . . . 'not mature enough' . . . "

"You are behaving like a naughty child, Anna. You know perfectly well that the critic was quite right . . . only he didn't see that you were tortured by the conductor. We can't have this sort of childishness. There is no time for it. You are going to sing now."

"I'll try," Anna held herself together through her tightly clasped hands, and this time her voice came through. At least she was making a sound, and the moment of panic had been overcome. But she was not singing from her whole being . . . something was held back still. She could not let out the strong full tone she could usually command at will. The room seemed small and constricting, the velvet curtains, always a little dusty, oppressed her.

"Can't we open a window?" she asked, as Protopova got up and came over to press her diaphragm.

"You are not breathing properly, Anna. I told you. Here," she said, pressing down hard, "the breath must come from *here*. You don't need air from a window, you need air inside your lungs. We really should not be having to struggle with such primary matters!"

Her head had been bent as she wrestled with Anna as a physical being. But then she looked up and let her hands fall and gave Anna a penetrating look.

"So, you are upset, Anna. But you can't let that, whatever it is, diminish Johann Sebastian Bach! When you enter this room you have to leave everything but the music behind!"

Protopova was apt to have the effect of a cold shower. The shock, the intensity of her being could, Anna had sometimes thought, break through rock. And under the attack, she finally laughed with relief.

"It is not a laughing matter."

"No, I was thinking, dear Protopova, that you are Orpheus, who could make the stones sing!"

"Now let us have a little glory, then," she said gleaming her teasing smile at Anna. "You have cracked open a little at last. I can tell you I have been working hard this morning. We can't afford to waste any more time." And they went back to the same passage. Anna took a deep breath and at last heard her voice soaring out, the good pressure inside her whole frame, the sense of power released.

"Well," Protopova said, taking out a handkerchief to wipe her hands, "that was better. But come here a moment . . . look, just there, don't be afraid to hold it. You seemed a fraction too quick—see, just there."

"I wish you were coming with me," Anna said.

"You don't need me. You will find Solti extremely patient and helpful."

"We have only one rehearsal."

"All the more reason to work hard before you go." And work hard they did, for another hour.

"Are you feeling better?" Protopova asked as Anna put on her coat.

"Yes, you wizard. Yes, I am." And Anna stooped to lift the old hand to her lips.

"You see, Bach is all that matters. What else is there?"

Anna walked down Newbury Street towards the French restaurant where she was meeting her mother, thinking about it, thinking about Protopova's capacity to serve music to the exclusion of everything else. For this electrifying bundle of energy and genius it was true. Music was her one consuming passion and she served it and had served it all her life with total dedication, expecting her pupils to do the same.

Was this possible if one was primarily a critic—and was it impossible for an interpreter? Even Protopova had noticed a change in Anna's voice in the first months of her marriage. "It comes from deeper," she had said. "It is *épanouie,* as the French would say."

Anna remembered blushing and then the austere Protopova had, for once, embraced her pupil. Ned had set her free, had made her feel wholly human. Now he was denying her humanity and censoring the being he had freed. How was she to handle that? How live with that?

Seated at a corner table in the restaurant opposite her mother, Anna ordered soup and a salad, but she was not hungry and when Teresa commented, she shook her head.

"I simply don't know how I shall do in Pittsburgh. I feel so tired today I can hardly walk. And Protopova was savage . . . rightly. I'm such a mess."

Teresa had had long experience of Anna's storm of nerves. It might seize her several days before a performance and that was best, for sometimes she seemed quite calm and then was suddenly paralyzed with fear in her dressing room just before the concert.

"You go through this every time, you know, when all the tension builds up, then is released in a marvelous way when you sing."

Anna shook her head and pushed her plate aside.

"Eat a mouthful. You're hungry after your lesson, only you don't know that yet."

"Oh Mama," Anna groaned, "I wish I could just disappear. Nothing feels right any more."

"It's Ned, I suppose," Teresa ventured. Since her marriage Anna had talked very little about Ned, but Teresa was quite aware that the euphoria of the first months had gone. She considered that was normal.

"I don't know. Maybe it's just me. Nothing I do is right."

"Marriage and a career such as yours are hard to manage in tandem, I expect. But you mustn't ask for the impossible. You are so intransigent, Anna."

"Am I?" Anna was astonished. She did not think of herself as intransigent. "I don't understand why Ned makes me so angry, why I can't accept him as he is."

"Does he accept you as you are?"

"Of course not. Everything about me irritates him."

"Everything?" Teresa lifted an eyebrow.

"He wants me to be the imaginary person he sees and hears when I sing, some kind of delightful songbird, who is never tired or cross, not a human being at all."

"If so, he is quite a foolish man." Teresa chuckled.

"I tried to talk about it with him the other day and he said I was two people, one possible and the other impossible, Jekyll and Hyde! That's crazy, Mama. The whole trouble is that I'm one person who reacts to everything that happens to me with all of myself! The loving one is also the angry one. Why can't he see that?"

But as her mother was silent, Anna twisted her glass of wine round and round slowly. One of the good things about their relation, Anna was thinking, was that they could be silent, and often were.

"It has always puzzled me," Teresa said finally, "why people fall in love with people so unlike themselves and then apparently can't be satisfied or happy till they have tried to change the other into a likeness of themselves. You used to think Ned was wonderful because he was so reserved, so sure of himself, so at home in the world. I remember you said, 'he makes me feel safe.' "

"I did?" Anna asked, amazed.

"Yes, you did, and I remember because it was one of the things that persuaded me he was the right man for you, my tempestuous, talented, insecure Anna!"

" 'At home in the world.' . . . Well he is, of course. But instead of making me feel safe, it makes me feel attacked.

I'll never be at home in his world, Mama. It's like a secret society. They take so much for granted—Ned does. He cannot imagine what insecurity is. . . . I don't mean financial insecurity, though that too. But for generations his family and his mother's have assumed that their way of doing things was the only way."

"Strange," Teresa said, "I think of Mrs. Fraser as a pathetic person—self-pitying, self-indulgent, under that disguise of good works and sweetness."

"Ned hates her. He says she ruined their childhood and made the children pay for her husband's death."

"That doesn't surprise me at all. But Anna," and now she looked at her daughter very seriously, "you really have no reason to feel insecure. Even in that world you are a personage, and surely 'they', whoever they are, recognize that."

"I suppose so."

"Ned is not a snob, Anna, at least from what I see of him he is not that. So what is the matter? Whatever your faults, your achievement is real."

"They don't have to achieve, you see. They just are. Oh mama, I want to feel loved not hated, protected not exposed to contempt!"

Teresa made no comment.

"I feel cursed, driven into a maze which has no way out, a prisoner of my own rage," Anna, having said it, realized that it was true and the truth frightened her.

"I have never thought it could be easy to be you," Teresa said. "Has it occurred to you that people who don't show anger are safe? When you let the anger out you expose yourself. Expose yourself to contempt, as you just suggested."

"But if I lock the anger up it turns into resentment. Ned can't see that. He can't see that that is what he does. He can't see that he is just as angry as I am, and he is punitive. I am not."

"Maybe not, but I expect he feels punished when you

scream at him. You are so violent, Anna."

"But his silence is violent, too—his coldness is punishing, Mama, Can't you see?" Anna had raised her voice, exasperated by her mother's appearing to take Ned's side. And Teresa winced.

"People are listening, Anna," she said in a low voice. "Please talk quietly. We are in a public place."

"You see, even you put me in the wrong," Anna whispered. And then because she loved her mother so much, she smiled, "I should be shot at dawn!" And the spell was broken, as they managed to laugh, laugh with each other at Anna's expense.

"Oh dear, if only I could laugh with Ned like that . . . The awful thing, Mama, is that we can never talk about anything quietly. He calls talking about anything to do with our relationship 'making a scene.' So the resentments build up again and again. . . . I do not see any way out of the maze."

"You are locked into two such different temperaments."

"So were you and father. How did you manage to stay together? How did you stand it, Mama?"

Teresa became actively silent for a moment. "Actively silent" was how Anna thought of it, for unlike Ned's silences that shut her out and walled her in, Teresa took Anna with her on the stream of her thoughts, and when she spoke after several minutes, Anna could join her and felt included.

"I suppose I gave in. For the sake of peace."

"I'll never do that," Anna said with absolute conviction. And again they laughed.

"No, I don't expect you ever will."

"I can't, Mama. My talent, whatever I have to give to life, is all bound up in my temperament—I have to be free to feel whatever I feel deeply enough, or it all goes sour inside me. I can't sing. Today, for instance, Protopova told me my voice was blurred . . . *blurred,* Mama!"

"Well, it didn't stay blurred, did it?"

"No."

"You see, you can handle it all when you put your mind onto it."

"It was scary for a while."

"Why do you suppose love and anger are so closely tied together?"

"Some terrible insecurity, some nakedness feels attacked. I do love Ned, you know that."

"Yes. Can't you try to take it a little easier, Anna, a short pause for station identification?"

"We'll have that. I'll be away in Pittsburgh at the end of the week. I guess we both look forward to being away from each other."

And as they said goodbye on Newbury Street, Anna reached out to take her mother's hand, "Thanks, Mama. What would I do without you?"

"I'm glad we could talk," Teresa answered. "And good luck, darling one!"

Chapter V

In the next few days, days of hard work with Protopova,
and as far as her marriage went, of limbo, of polite surface
and no communication, Anna was struck by the fact that
wherever she went and whatever newspaper she read or
news on TV she watched, anger met her like a leitmotif.
Bombs were thrown on innocent civilians, children took
up shotguns and shot their parents dead, husbands beat
their wives, a couple murdered a small child by beating
him to death. There were even grotesque examples of it
as when a man in a car rammed another car which had
cut in on him and severely injured its occupant! Had it
always been like this? Was anger an ineradicable part of
the human race? Had it to do with unfulfilled lives
screaming for help? And in other times were there perhaps ritual ways of dealing with it? A formal duel; knights
jousting; a priest called in to exorcize the devil? Was the
Victorian lady's way of handling it to take to her bed and
become an invalid?

Anna's mood after her talk with her mother was one of
remorse and dissatisfaction with herself. Her verbal bra-
vado about her own anger had given way to a pervading
sense of guilt. Somewhere along the way she had come
upon a Quaker pamphlet which contained the words

"Love is the hardest lesson." Why had she and Ned allowed their love to be poisoned? Who was responsible? She thought these thoughts as she walked to and fro to Protopova's for her lessons which had become intense and exhausting as they always did in the last days before a performance.

Ned was out at the Tavern Club on Tuesday and had a meeting on the Wednesday before she was to leave. So they hardly met and, when they did, exchanged banalities. It did not help that Ned appeared to be perfectly happy to do so, relieved, she suspected, that the passionate exchanges had gone underground for the time being.

But she herself did not shut Ned out. In some ways she was more aware of him, more connected to him than ever before. The anger which had seized her like a bolt of lightning was now working its way down into another layer of her being and forcing her to think things out. And it was now not Ned as much as herself whom she felt forced to confront.

On an impulse she called Ernesta Aldrich, one of the very few of Ned's friends with whom she felt at ease. After all, it was Ernesta who had dragged Ned to hear her sing and who was thus responsible for her marriage. She could, Anna felt, be trusted. And also she understood something about what it was to be Anna Lindstrom. For when Anna asked if she would come for lunch, Ernesta's response was, "I wouldn't think of it. You have enough on your mind without fussing about in the kitchen. You come here. Pursey will fix something light and we can talk in peace. It's been ages . . . "

"Thanks, Ernesta. I'll come right after my lesson at noon, or a little after."

And there she was, sitting on the sofa by the fire, feeling like an exhausted swimmer who had come to land.

"You are looking beautiful, Anna. You've lost weight. It's becoming."

"I've been working frightfully hard. And in my usual panic before a concert . . . the Bach *B-Minor Mass* in Pittsburgh on Saturday."

"How kind of you then to come and see me. I am flattered."

"Oh Ernesta," Anna said, flinging the amenities aside, "I needed to see you!"

"I'm even more flattered. Dubonnet, my dear?" Ernesta poured out, took a sip, and waited. "Well, what's on your mind?"

"Ned's on my mind!"

"Such a curious creature," Ernesta said, smiling. "But he has a saving grace, his passion for music—would you agree?"

"I sometimes wonder whether music is not a frustrating passion."

"Why?"

"Because . . . because it makes people long for something they can't have, something that cannot be translated into life."

Ernesta thought this over. "What you are telling me is that Ned's passion for music was translated into a passion for you? Why not? He seems to have what he wanted, lucky man."

"You don't marry a voice, Ernesta!"

"No," Ernesta said, lowering her eyes, "I don't suppose you do." And as Anna was silent, Ernesta looked up and met her eyes. "What did Ned marry? A wonderfully warm woman full of life, spontaneous joy, laughter."

"Don't." Anna was close to tears because Ernesta could say all that and mean it, but Ned did not see it. "Ned married a fury . . . that's what he thinks," and she added, "and he has almost persuaded me that is true."

"You mustn't let him," Ernesta said, quite firmly.

"I do have an awful temper, and letting anger out is what you must never never do according to Ned."

"I'll tell you something, Anna. The day I took him to your concert he was quite lit up at lunch afterwards. He talked very violently about his mother, and for a second I thought I saw that for him deep feeling comes clothed in anger. It was a puzzling insight, but I did sense that. Maybe that's why he is so afraid of it."

"But he's so controlled, so cold, Ernesta."

"He's seething inside."

"Yes," Anna said immensely relieved to hear it said, "I know."

"Why did you marry him, Anna? May I ask that, since we are talking openly? I have often wondered."

Anna laughed, "It's ludicrous. I married him because he seemed so strong, so sure of himself, so comfortable in the world. I felt in some obscure way like an orphan suddenly adopted, suddenly safe after years of struggle and insecurity."

"Why is that ludicrous? It seems rather sensible, rather unexpectedly sensible of you!"

"It's ludicrous because what he does is to undermine any security I have in myself, to see that I am always put in the wrong, to bait me into wild rages with his coldness, his withdrawals, his sneers . . . that's why."

"Why do you let him do it?" Ernesta probed. "You are a powerful woman, Anna. And you are someone in the world."

"Oh, I know," Anna brushed all that aside. "But what follows on anger for me is despair. And then I can't sing. I feel undone." She had been about to say "castrated" but she was not, after all, a man.

"Have you considered divorce?"

"Lately, yes." But even as she said it Anna had to withdraw it. "No, not really. I can't imagine it. You see, Ernesta, the war between us goes very deep. I can't walk out on something so unsolved and so painful. I love Ned."

"And does he love you?"

"I don't know. Sometimes I think he does. But he is so afraid of feeling. He can't handle it. It terrifies him. Why?" Before Ernesta could answer Anna added, "You can't imagine what a relief it is to talk to someone . . . someone from Ned's world, someone who understands him, is fond of him, who can help." Anna's eyes had filled with tears. "I feel so helpless."

"I wish I could help," Ernesta said thoughtfully. "Somewhere along the way something must have happened to close him off. It may be that his father's death had something to do with it."

"But surely love should be able to open the door."

"Dear Anna, you are an optimist." Ernesta hesitated but then evidently decided to be frank. "What if the door opens and there is nothing there?"

"I don't believe that. You have only to see Ned with Fonzi to know that isn't true."

"Who is Fonzi?" Ernesta asked, clearly astonished.

"The dachshund—not a male friend!" And this last brought laughter and an alleviation of the intensity of the last minutes.

"Oh, a dog . . . but can't you see, dogs are safe. His father was crazy about dogs, you know. It runs in the family."

"For the same reason, no doubt," Anna said bitterly.

"So, you are a little jealous of Fonzi . . . I don't blame you."

"Not jealous. But every time Ned talks to him in that tender voice, it hurts. Never has he shown tenderness to me." Now Anna did not try to keep the tears back. She wept unashamedly. At least Ernesta would not despise her tears, she thought and said so after she had blown her nose.

"Well," Ernesta said in her practical voice, "that is no news. All men wince at a woman's tears. It's in the genes." And she added, "My husband simply cleared out and left the house when I cried. They take it as an assault, an unfair weapon, and act accordingly."

"Why is it unfair to be upset? Why is it feeling, almost *any* feeling, if expressed, is an assault? That's what I can't understand. Ned won't even talk about it quietly after we have a fight. He says things like 'We have had one scene already'!"

At this Ernesta laughed, "I can hear him saying that! Come along, dear Anna, we had better have something to eat. Pursey's soufflé will fall."

"I'll just go and wash and be right back."

But over the coffee when they were back again by the fire, Anna, relieved by having been able to talk and to feel she could be herself without the ever-present censor, said gently, "You know, Ernesta, I am rather a handful for Ned to cope with. And sometimes I think the war is really between one ethos and another. I'm half Italian as you know and the Boston ethos gives me the creeps. It's so cramped, so the opposite of life-enhancing. . . . But on the other hand the volubility, the quick changes of mood, the spontaneity just strike Ned as somehow faked or superficial. He doesn't know how hard I think about it all, how deep he forces me to go."

"Ah!" Ernesta smiled, "Now I have a clue as to why you love him! I see so many marriages with no depth at all, only a surface compatibility—habit has taken over. You grow. Dear Anna, what a great woman you are!"

"I'm a great fool, that's for sure. And now, I really must leave you in peace."

"I'm afraid I haven't been much help. I have no solutions to offer."

"No . . . I suspect there are none. But you've been an enormous help."

Standing now, the two women embraced each other. Then Ernesta just touched Anna's cheek. "You're going to give a great performance, my dear." Then she gave Anna a quizzical look, "And maybe that's what this difficult marriage is all about, as far as you are concerned, anyway."

Protopova was pleased with Anna's progress and Anna herself knew that her voice, her true power had come back. It was tremendously exciting to let go again, to be able to send her voice soaring, to have gotten rid of the censor. Often after the lesson she walked for an hour simply to calm down, ending in the Public Gardens on a bench. There, with a pocketful of peanuts for the squirrels, she sat, alive to every tremor of wind in the leaves and alive in the same way to what was happening in herself.

It was a little like climbing a mountain. At times the summit was not even in sight; at times it suddenly appeared out of the clouds, miles away. Would she ever reach the free air, the great composing view?

One thing was becoming clear. That anger was not one solid block or rock but several blocks that had little or no relation to each other. When Ned said, "You were always angry, even as a small child," he had been right. And that anger, those sudden explosions that broke out, seemingly about nothing, were what troubled her most. They caused guilt and remorse. With Teresa she could laugh and say "I should be shot at dawn", but under the laughter there was shame.

Why am I like that? Anna asked herself, watching two squirrels chattering with rage over a peanut. A very slight frustration could light the fuse toward anger . . . why did it seem uncontrollable at times? To blow up about nothing? Why, at thirty-six, had she not come to terms with that demon?

She remembered the short fuse over the arrangement of flowers on the weekend. But then Ned had also been angry. They had let a small thing grow into a big thing. So where was the small thing rooted? From where had it drawn its force?

Anna instinctively blamed herself after a scene like that, but she was becoming aware lately that it was not as much a question of taking blame as of understanding that below an extreme temperamental rift there was a less accessible war going on, and that was the crux of the matter. And what was that war all about?

The masculine in each of them at war with the feminine in each of them? She was, she couldn't help being, as her mother had said, a powerful personality, with a strong compulsive drive to succeed, to dominate in her profession. That, she supposed, was the masculine side of her, or some people would define it as that. Whereas Ned, so obtuse in some ways, at his worst what she thought of as a stupid sensibility, unable to connect with anything outside his rigid ethos or even to examine it rationally, was extremely sensitive when it came for instance to flowers, to paintings, to music—in that whole area of his being, he was using the feminine in him and had apparently made his peace with that. At the other end of the spectrum, his fleeing any attempt to talk about feeling, his running for cover, or turning to attack, when feeling was demanded —that, she presumed might be called masculine. He permitted feeling only in relation to Fonzi! And in a flash of insight she realized that Ned really disliked the woman in her, disliked her need for tender words, despised her tears and took her anger always as some kind of aberration.

And each was fighting the other off to defend, to keep intact that adamant central self which seemed threatened. So in the end Anna came to see—and it was painful —that there was both murder and suicide in their love. He called out the violence in her and she in him, for his withdrawals and cold punishment were certainly violent in their way. And afterward she at least felt suicidal. And what did he feel? She had no idea. Never once had he let her into his deepest self. What is the matter with him, Anna thought? What wounds that cannot be healed? Where did it all begin?

All Anna knew for sure was that when she could sing as she had that morning, the conflicting powers could be

gathered together and freed, and when she and Ned
made love she had sometimes had the same feeling of a
breakthrough, of the warring selves gathered together in
a tension that broke at the orgasm. She had asked herself
many times whether the anger was not part of the sexual
act between her and Ned. Breaking out of the prison
together. Now what was happening was that there was no
longer any moment when the tension could break. There
was no "we." They had become separated antagonists in
an icy landscape.

When Ned left for the office on the Friday of her departure Anna was packing in the bedroom.

"Well, I'm off," he said in the doorway.

Anna stood with a nightgown in her hands, and waited
for him to wish her luck. She waited perhaps five seconds,
looking at him in disbelief. When he was still silent, just
standing there, she said, "You might at least wish me luck,
Ned."

"You don't need it."

At that moment Anna felt such pressure in her head
that she was afraid of cracking into pieces. She bent over
the suitcase and folded her nightgown carefully and laid
it there. She heard the door close and Fonzi bark. Then
she burst into tears of sheer fury and frustration. "You
beast," she murmured, "you cold, mean beast!" But she
knew she could not afford tears, not now, not with a concert forty-eight hours away, not with a rehearsal at five
that afternoon. She went on packing and forced the tears
back. When she was ready to leave she called her mother.

"Ned wouldn't even wish me luck, Mama," she said in
a perfectly controlled voice.

"You must put Ned out of your mind, Anna," said her
mother firmly. "You will go and give a great performance.
This, your talent, is your own responsibility and gift."

"It's so lonely, Mama."

"Of course it is, of course. Every performer is absolutely alone when it comes to the crunch. You've always been alone, dear, and you always will be."

"It didn't matter when I was really alone. Now I feel torn in two. Beaten."

"Stop it, Anna. You can't afford this."

"I have to go," Anna was suddenly in a panic.

"Good luck, Anna"

"Thanks. I needed to hear that."

On the plane Anna felt a surge of relief and as they circled Boston and she looked down for a moment on the Public Gardens, she was happy to be cut off from all the pain, on her way to her own real life, to that stage, that orchestra and Bach, whom—she felt it in her chest where her voice lay like some great animal waiting for its release —she would serve well.

Chapter VI

Ned, too, took the days he would have alone as a reprieve. It was a positive pleasure to come home that night to Fonzi whose mood was always joyful and welcoming, without having to respond to accusations or tears, and without feeling guilty because he could not respond.

When they came back from the ritual walk around the Common before Ned poured himself a Scotch and looked at the news, it was bliss to put his feet up, light a pipe and settle in to an evening's read. He didn't get his supper until after eight.

"Perfect peace with loved ones far away," Ned said aloud, "eh, Fonzi?" and Fonzi wagged his tail. Fonzi was a good listener. He liked to hear Ned's voice and Ned found himself telling Fonzi things, thinking aloud, a more companionable thing than sitting there inside his own mind, silent.

"I'm not a cruel beast, Fonzi, am I?" How could she not understand that you can't force people to talk about their feelings? He couldn't do it. When he saw that look in Anna's eyes, that furious yet imploring look so close to tears and heard the edge in her voice, he simply closed down all the hatches, took in the sails, and waited like a sailor in a small boat before a sudden storm. Yes, that is what it was like. Anna was a primal force, a hurricane. He had thought he was marrying a loving, natural woman who would be friendly and warm, a good companion. He knew her career was important. He honored her for that. But he certainly did not foresee an endless war, no holds barred! "What does she want, Fonzi? Absolute capitulation? A slave? Nothing but praise and adoration? God knows she gets plenty of *that.*"

Fonzi, sensing a change of tone, sensing anger, got up and came over to lick Ned's ankle.

"It's all right, Fonzi, I'm not fussing at you! You are a good dog, an excellent fellow," and Ned scratched Fonzi between the ears. Then, gentled by his own action, Ned sighed. He put his hands behind his neck and gazed at the ceiling. "I should have wished her luck, Fonzi. That was mean, but I couldn't help it. She says I can't give, but can't she see that I take all that for granted, Fonzi? Married people shouldn't have to be praised and petted all the time, should they? Anna is not a dog, after all. You do have to be petted, don't you, Fonzi? You have to feel connected to a hand, I suppose."

But Fonzi had fallen fast asleep and was lying on his back, his long ears flopped awry in a charming abandon. And Ned became silent. Some things he really could not say aloud, even to Fonzi.

Those things which had to do with sex, Ned always managed to chase away. Like furies at the window, they could be driven off and must be driven off. Even thinking about sex seemed to Ned embarrassing and to be avoided at all cost. It was something to be done in silence and in the dark and never exposed to a word, even a word of love or tenderness. It was deeply buried, the unmentionable secret, like death itself, and indeed sex sometimes seemed like a death to Ned. A black-out of everything he associated with a rational being.

"Come on, Fonzi, let's eat," he said, giving a huge yawn as he pulled himself up, a yawn of hunger and of distaste.

Anna was always talking about being fully human and

accused him of being able to compartmentalize himself.
Well, why not? Only God could tell why "Love has
pitched his mansion in the place of excrement"! The line
had haunted him since he studied Yeats at Exeter. It was
really rather disgusting when you came to think about it,
so better not think about it.

"At best titillating, at worst shameful, Fonzi."

Ned ate his supper, a casserole and salad left for him by
Felicia, the maid, who came in every day to tidy up and
to walk Fonzi before she left at noon. He put on a record,
a Mozart concerto for flute and harp, and let himself be
transported into that elegant, poignant world where no
one was angry and no one felt anything below the belt, at
least not Ned, who had always hated Wagner because of
the disturbing effect he had "on the lower animal" as
Ned's mother put it. Ned had felt justified in his inherent
dislike of Wagner since Wagner was the Nazis' em-
blematic composer. And from there he was suddenly
aware of Anna, the musician, Anna with the perfect taste,
the delicacy, the control she could summon when she was
singing. Anna whom he had once adored, whom he had
wanted so desperately to know, to be with, to marry,
Anna who at this moment—Ned looked at his watch—was
perhaps on her way back to her hotel after the rehearsal,
Anna who had been singing Bach.

She could still send a shiver down his spine when she
sang, when she was in absolute control, invulnerable, way
outside and beyond the messy, disturbing personal world.
And Ned realized that he still loved her power but that
he found everything about her as a woman distasteful.
Why did women cry so much? Why were they always
talking about feeling? Why did Anna have to attack him
all the time about his "ethos" as though it were some
primitive armor he wore that she felt compelled to tear
off to get at *him.*

What she could not seem to understand was that she
would never get at him that way, or perhaps in any way.

He could not deal with irrational impulse—her physical attacks outraged him. If I did what she wanted, if I gave myself away as she does, I would cease to exist. Muddling about with the soul makes me sick. Something has to be kept safe. From what?

From being destroyed.

Chapter VII

In fact the rehearsal had gone very well, almost too well, for there was always the danger that the peak had been reached too soon, before the performance itself. Solti had embraced her as she was leaving the concert hall and said, "Do that tomorrow night, cara Anna, and all will be well!"

Anna called room service for a chicken sandwich, hot milk, and a double Scotch, then walked up and down for a few minutes, went to the window to look down on the lights of the city, and a few cars flashing by in the rain. She felt exhilarated and restless, for a second thought of calling Ned—but to say what? No, instead she sat down at the desk—room service was apt to be terribly slow—and wrote the letter she had been thinking about all week.

Dear Ned,

This is almost the only letter I have ever written you but I need to try to communicate with you after so much misunderstanding and anger lately. Please try to read this as from a gentle unblurred voice—it is very bad that we cannot talk. I know it is partly my fault. My quick temper freezes you into silence, a silence that seems to be becoming a permanent armor which you cannot or will not take off.

You lay the burden of guilt upon me when you insist that I

am simply an angry person and have been so since childhood. There is some truth in this but it is not the *whole* truth, Ned. I think you too are an angry person—I sometimes wonder whether everyone is not born angry, furious at having been torn out of warmth and safety and suddenly alone in what must seem a harsh cold world at the very start. But you were taught or learned quickly to bury your anger, to refuse to allow it out, and you have come to believe that if you do not show it, if you never let it out, that it is really not there. Your brother seems to have handled his anger by learning to attack first, to be always the attacker to preserve himself from attack—is that it with Paul? My anger leaps out like a real demon and is terribly damaging to others—and to me. I am afterward filled with guilt and remorse and feel I am always in the wrong. But I have to admit that these sudden pounces out of the blue do break the tension for me and there is some part of me that recognizes that letting anger out rather than burying it is healthy. You will resist this idea with all your being. I suppose I am writing this letter to beg you to consider your own anger, not to deny that it exists. We each have a demon or daimon, as it is sometimes called, only we handle it in opposite ways and maybe that is why we seem to be in a state of unremitting war. But, Ned, you show your anger by coldness, by withdrawing from me, by *not* giving, and if only you could see that this is perhaps as punishing as my violence, we might be able to make a bridge. It was cruel of you not to wish me luck when I left you. It was, if you like, as punishing as a slap in the face. But because it was an example of "not doing," it did not seem bad or cruel to you. Please try to think about this.

You never use the word "love"; you can never use an endearment with me as you do a hundred times a day with Fonzi. Why? Why can't you tell me in words what you are feeling, except a cold rebuke now and then? I flare up and then very quickly come back to you with love—or I used to, until that day when I kissed your hand and you said—you did say it, Ned— "abject!" That day something froze up in me and is still frozen.

Now I come to the hardest part of this letter. But I must try to talk about it with you now, or our marriage will wither as so many we see around us have withered, for one reason or another. Not, I think, for *this* reason. There is something in you which cannot accept yourself as a sexual being. When we first made love I was so wholly with you and felt so whole in myself that I hardly noticed that you never *say* anything. Sex perhaps is your demon as anger is mine . . . that is, it pounces on you, and under its power you do things that you cannot face in daylight. I have used the word "compartmentalize" before. It shocks and hurts me terribly that you cannot make love to me in freedom and joy. Can't you see that this turns me into a prostitute? The vehicle for an act for which you do not feel responsible and which your reason cannot accept?

I want to give you my whole self and take your whole self into me, Ned. But perhaps this is what frightens and turns you off most of all! You are quick to sneer at what seems to you sentimental or weak, but for me—how can I put it into words?—sex must be metaphysical, a true communion, or it is indeed bestiality and nothing else. Maybe we are each rather old-fashioned but once more in opposite ways. Your mother must have instilled into you that some things were "not nice." You are afraid of your own sensuality, so again I am punished by something negative, something which *denies me* as a whole human being. I feel frustrated in the deepest sense and humiliated, too. So I get angry.

I infuriate you because I demand something you cannot give or refuse yourself as well as me. It seems to me therefore to go deeper than mere irritation, than the clash of two temperaments at opposite poles. It is a question of marriage itself, Ned. As far as I can see we are not married. Whatever all this means to you when you read it, you must realize that I love you, and I must believe that you love me.

Ned, please read this with your heart, not as the prehistoric animal who hides itself away.

                                                          Anna

It had taken an hour, and then at last the boy came with her sandwich and milk and Scotch. Anna was very hungry, but not, as she had hoped she might be, relieved by writing to Ned. She had, she realized, only set up another tension, that of waiting for his response. But at least it was done. She had straightened it out in her own mind and that unknotted one knot that night, the knot that communication with him was not possible. And very soon after she got into bed, Anna was fast asleep.

Chapter VIII

Teresa called while Anna was having her breakfast in bed, and Anna was able to tell her that she had slept well, that the rehearsal had gone almost too well, and that she was feeling quite calm.

"I'll go for a walk later on. The rain has stopped, I see."

But when Anna put the receiver down she felt the day ahead would be interminable, a day of walking on eggs, holding everything in balance and not allowing panic to move in. She read the paper with close attention, even the business pages which she usually shirked. Then she lay there for an hour prolonging the moment when she would have to dress and go out.

She reread her letter to Ned, decided to tear it up, and then decided to mail it, and went out in her wrapper to let it fall down the shoot by the elevators. Would it do any good? What good for waves to beat against rock? For the next hours Anna knew she must shut Ned out, so she got up and dressed. She suddenly remembered there was to be an interview at noon. A woman reporter was being sent over from the paper she had just been reading.

She dressed carefully in a black suit with a white ruffly blouse, examined herself in the mirror, wondering whether she should have her hair done again. It looked quite all right, those massed black curls had held well, but it would be something to do later on . . . only what if the hotel hairdresser wrecked it? No, too nerve-wracking, Anna decided.

It all seemed trivial suddenly. And she imagined Ned in a meeting, no doubt, with men who had real power in their hands, while she, Anna Lindstrom was about to waste a day simply trying to control her nerves. Absurd. Then she heard Protopova's voice, "Bach, absurd? That is blasphemy!" And Anna told herself, looking quite severely at the face in the mirror, that whatever might be trivial about her, at least she served something greater than herself as best she could. She lifted her chin and laughed at the solemn face in the mirror. What fools we mortals be!

Three baskets of flowers were delivered. One had a spray of orchids in a charming rectangular glass. The card was signed with a woman's name that Anna did not recognize, "Homage to Anna Lindstrom." The second was a round bowl of pink roses, rather sweet, Anna thought and smiled as she read the card, for it was from a former schoolmate at Juilliard who had married and given up her career. "I'll be there tonight applauding you." Dear Nancy! Anna seemed to remember that she had four or five children and adored her husband, a pediatrician. The third was a huge formal basket of glads from the management and Anna hid it in a corner . . . she had always hated glads, even the name.

But the flowers had started the whole machinery of anticipation and tension in motion and Anna felt happy, felt, she described it to herself, like an empty glass which was beginning to be filled with that intoxicating liquor of performance ahead. That was what Ned simply could not imagine when he said things like "You don't need luck!" She desperately needed every reassurance she could get! And flowers always gave her a tremendous lift. In the impersonal hotel room which, like all hotel rooms, destroyed identity rather than recognizing its existence, the flowers told Anna Lindstrom who she was.

She was glad to open the door at noon to a young woman in peasant skirt, high black boots, and a long mass of fuzzy hair which looked as though it had never been combed, and who seemed to Anna absurdly young.

"You have so many flowers," she said looking around dismayed and holding a single red rose wrapped in cellophane awkwardly, as she laid her big satchel down, "I brought you a rose."

"Thank you, my dear. That is sweet of you."

"Do you mind if I use a tape recorder?"

"Not at all. Sit down and set it and I'll just put the rose in water . . . we can't let it fade," and Anna went into the bathroom. Of course the rose was much too long to fit in the hotel glass, but Anna managed to cut it with nail scissors and brought it back and set it on the small table beside the two armchairs where they would be talking. "There!" she said sitting down. "Now, what can I say? What do you want to know, Miss Springhof?"

"I just have to be sure this is working," and the girl played back Anna's questions, which sounded now rather loud and very self-conscious.

"I do sound pretentious, don't I?"

"No, oh no—you have such a wonderful voice!"

"Do I?" Anna smiled. "You know on the day of a performance I am always in a state of terror for fear I shall wake up with no voice at all!"

"Has that ever happened?"

"No, but it might . . . it's like having an eccentric animal inside that may rebel," and Anna laughed, then added, "Seriously, it's nerve wracking to be one's own instrument, so to speak."

"But you are looking forward to the concert? It's sold out, you know."

"Is it? Oh dear . . . that's scary. But of course it is always thrilling to be part of such a tremendous work and to be

singing under Solti with a great orchestra, and with such
a star as Madame Elgar at my side."

"You have sung with her before?"

"No, but we got along famously at the rehearsal yesterday afternoon. She was extremely kind to me. I feel honored to be singing with her."

"People say she is losing her voice."

"Nonsense! People don't know what they are talking
about. Lotte Lehmann was still wonderful at sixty!" Anna
felt passionately about this and showed it, "The very people who have adored and applauded a singer for years,
seem to be lying in wait for her to fail, seem to get some
sort of kick out of a diminishing talent. It's horrible. I
sometimes hate the audience. It's like some beast one has
to go in and kill. Caruso felt that, you know. He said it was
like being a matador and having to kill a bull."

"But you don't feel that, do you?"

"Yes, I do. Every single performer is exposed to the
possibility of jeers—but of course one forgets that once
the music is there. It's worse in a concert when one goes
out alone. That agonizing moment of confrontation."

"Wow!" said Miss Springhof. "I never thought it was
like that."

"You won't publish your question about Madame Elgar,
will you? She does not deserve that comment about failing
powers. Promise me, you will cut that out?"

"I promise," Miss Springhof looked at her notes. "Anyway the interview is about you, Mrs. Lindstrom."

"If it's Mrs., then it is Mrs. Fraser. Otherwise, Anna
Lindstrom, please."

"I'm sorry. You are married? I didn't know."

"Yes, I married Ned Fraser two years ago. We live in
Boston."

"You have children?"

"No." It was said with such finality that there was an
inevitable pause. Miss Springhof was obviously daunted

and did not know quite what to say next. "You want to ask whether I want children, I expect."

"Well . . . maybe . . . I suppose it's hard to combine a career like yours with a family, but . . . "

"I'm accused of being much too frank," she laughed, "but we're on earth such a short time, why not be honest? What will it matter in two hundred years? I'm thirty-six years old and I am on the brink of real fame, on the brink of being able at last to choose what I shall sing and where and when. I can't afford to stop now and take time off. So the answer is that one has to make choices and I made a choice long ago, long before I married Ned."

"I see, of course." Miss Springhof looked doubtful.

"Somehow we are taught in America that we can have everything: a career, children, everything. A woman who becomes a nun gives up all idea of having a family . . . and I suppose a career taken seriously implies some sacrifice."

"You don't seem like a nun at all," Miss Springhof smiled out from under her hair.

"Oh, I'm not. The impurity, the passion, the rage even —they are all there. That animal inside me, my voice, has to cope with them all!" And Anna laughed. "You see!"

But of course Miss Springhof did not see and could have no idea, and when Anna suggested that she herself must now rest and saw the young girl to the door, she felt as usual that she had made a fool of herself. Interviews were always dangerous because to make it worth the interviewer's time you had to try at least to be interesting and being interesting too often meant confidences.

Anna put on her coat and went out for a walk to calm down. The sun had come out and it was a cool, brilliant day. She spent an hour browsing in a bookstore and came away with a paperback of Rilke letters and a novel of Eudora Welty's she had always meant to read. Then she was ravenously hungry—why did bookstores have this effect?—and by great good luck found a small Italian restaurant. There she ate a plate of ravioli and drank a glass of wine. Strange how a small piece of luck could appear on such a day as an augury. All would be well.

And in the remaining hours before she must bathe and dress, Anna knew she was on the beam. Dread had given way to expectation, and her only moment of panic was at seven when she could not get the zipper up of her dress. "Don't do this to me," she said to the dress, and finally it gave in. Anna then looked herself over in the mirror. . . . "Of course I am too fat," she thought, then she remembered that Ned had told her he couldn't stand what he called clotheshorse women. And she remembered also that beside Madame Elgar she was a sylph. "Such vanity," she scolded herself, "Get on with it, Anna. It's Bach now, not Anna Lindstrom who matters."

And in the dressing room she and Sophie Elgar joked and waited, wished each other good luck, joked some more. "I'm always afraid I'll burst out of my dress, aren't you?" Sophie said, smoothing herself down for the twentieth time. "Then," she laughed aloud, "there I am, immense, but I suddenly feel tiny in front of that huge orchestra. You know, it really takes weight, Anna, to put a voice out over the orchestra!"

And then the knock at the door and they were making their way out onto the stage on a ripple of applause. It died out and there was a second of silence, then the chorus seemed almost to lift the roof with the *Kyrie* and Anna felt freed, lifted out of herself on the power and glory of it. She clasped her hands. They were ice cold. Then it was time to turn the page before her, take a deep breath, and summon her voice. And it was there! Oh, the effort as though she were throwing her voice like a discus as far as it would go, soaring out beyond her. Oh, the supreme effort she felt right down to her feet! The thrill of blending with, then separating from Sophie's soprano, of battling the orchestra, an ocean of sound behind them! It seemed only a long moment before her solo, *"Que sedes ad dexteram Patris, miserere nobis,"* and her voice was there interweaving with the flute, as serene and pure as the flute. When it was over, she closed her eyes, unaccountably close to tears, remembering Protopova and all she had done to make it as perfect as they could make it together. The phrasing, the long breath needed had been there at her command, better than ever before.

No concert appearances alone could ever bring this joy, this ecstasy of being a part of such a company of instruments and voices in the service of Bach. Solti was pulling it out of them all, pulling it together with such grace!

And now he was turning to Sophie and her for their duet and Anna felt the joy of the two voices singing with and against each other in a glorious interweaving. *"Et in unum Dominum . . . "* No rehearsal could give any idea of what the performance, this performance, was to be. Worth all the work, all those hours with Protopova, all the anxiety, to have this power and to be able to use it well.

At the end of the performance Anna felt she had been in heaven. The soloists were called back five times but they all knew that what had happened was the result of a union of all their gifts. And in the dressing room Sophie embraced Anna and said, "My dear, what a great night it was!"

It was.

When Nancy came backstage, she was in tears. "Oh Anna, you were so marvelous. I don't know why I'm crying!"

"It's that music—what Bach does!" And Anna pulled Nancy out into the green room where they could sit down and talk. "Where's John?"

He had been shy about coming backstage and was waiting in the auditorium, Nancy explained. "It's worth everything, to be able to do that—to be part of it, isn't it?" she asked, "I envy you!"

"Not with four children, you don't!"

"Well, I suppose there are compensations for not making it," she admitted.

"You haven't changed a bit, Nancy. How we used to laugh, do you remember?"

But Nancy was taking Anna in and hardly responded to this. "You have changed, Anna."

"How? How have I changed? I feel just the same, just as much a fool as ever!"

"Do you still cry at the drop of a hat?"

"Oh yes! The Italian is still very much in the ascendant."

"But you seem not older exactly, but rounder," and as Anna giggled, she amended it, "That's not what I meant."

"I'm much too fat, but that's no change."

"No, I meant, rounded out inside, mature, I suppose . . . happiness does it. You must be very happy. Somehow I had imagined you would never marry."

"Happiness?" Anna was taken by surprise by the word and what it obviously implied.

"I wish I could meet your husband."

"Ned is a very funny man."

"He makes you laugh?"

"No, he makes me furious."

"I get awfully cross with John sometimes . . . " But this was not the place or the time to talk about marriage and Anna changed the subject by asking about Nancy's children.

Finally, since Nancy was clearly nervous about keeping John waiting, they said goodbye. They had never been intimate but felt the impulse to do more than shake hands, and ended by kissing each other warmly on each cheek. "I hate to let you go . . . " Anna said. "Old friend."

"Whatever happens, Anna, you've done something tremendous with your life. You're going to be a great star. Don't let them get you down, honey."

"I won't," Anna said.

But back in the hotel she felt so empty and so alone that she simply lay down fully dressed on the bed. Ned, Ned, she tried to fill the emptiness with his name, but it didn't help. Finally she called her mother. "I was absolutely transported by the music, Mama. I've never done better. Everyone was wonderful."

"You don't sound exactly happy," Teresa said.

"No."

"Well, you're having a reaction I expect. You'd better order some supper sent up and then get a good night's sleep."

"I think I'll stay over one more day, go to the museum maybe. I think I need a day all by myself, without tension."

"That's a good idea."

"Maybe you could call Ned before eight-thirty tomorrow. Tell him I'll be home Tuesday and could we go out for dinner."

"Why don't you call him yourself?"

"Oh, he'll be asleep now, and I might not be awake tomorrow morning. Tell him the concert was a triumph," she added.

She did not tell her mother that she wanted Ned to read her letter before she saw him again. That had been the real reason, but nevertheless a day without obligations, a day of solitude, of not having to respond to anyone or ask anything of herself proved to be a good plan.

The papers came with her breakfast and the reviews were all right. There was a flattering mention in one of her duet with Sophie. "The two voices seemed to be in perfect harmony, neither dominating the other. Bach was well served." A crumb, but at least not a poisoned crumb. Relieved, relaxed at last, Anna lay there, watching the sunlight make a broad band on the yellow wall, and for the first time in months thought about Ned without wincing and without anger. Perhaps she had fallen in love two years before, with that closed handsome face just because it was a foreign country to be discovered, to be made hers, a compelling mystery to come to understand . . . only she had not come to understand. And what had touched her at first, the loneliness of the man, his inability to relate, to give, later became what she hated and fought. "Oh Ned," she murmured, "Ned . . ."

Had he also fallen in love with what he came to hate, that had grown to be simply irritation? Her exuberance, her quick changes from joy to grief, from laughter to rage? No, he had fallen in love with a performer not a woman at all. What had he imagined then? Capturing a singing bird and putting it in a cage? What had he *expected?* Damned if I know, Anna thought.

She wondered then if passionate love was always like this, whether all marriages became a frightful war where each partner was determined to change the other and, if the marriage lasted, simply came to accept the unacceptable, gave up. That was true of Paul and Hilda, she imagined. But perhaps they had stuck it out for the sake of the children . . .

Here Anna got out of bed. Children? A child? Last night she had for a moment envied Nancy, secure in her family, but that was once more to long for the normal, the acceptable, to be like everyone else, to feel justified. How could a childless woman feel justified?

"But I do when I sing!" Anna said aloud. "I do!" She looked at herself in the mirror as she pulled off her nightgown. That broad chest, the full breasts, the strong throat were all there for a purpose, to have the power to project a voice, to be the exact sound box that was needed. And she felt for a second exultant, rejoicing in a gift, in the flesh itself. Oh, why couldn't Ned make love seeing what he desired? Why always in the dark?

The thought forced her to get dressed and go out. By now he would have her letter. Pulling on her stockings, Anna was shaking. She felt the sweat on her upper lip, the signature of panic. What if I never went back? What if I ran away?

In the same instant she had an impulse to get on a plane and go back at once. No, Anna, she told herself. Take this

day and use it well. Use it to achieve composure for once.
But how did one do that? With everything in a whirl of
questions without answers inside her? One did it if one
could by taking refuge in art. I'll sing the *Kindertoten
Lieder* at that concert next month, she thought, and during this day she would plan the program, a morning musicale at a club in Dallas. She would go back with her mind
made up, with something accomplished, whatever Ned
did in answer to her letter. She would go home as Anna
Lindstrom not Anna Fraser.

Anna Lindstrom spent the morning at the art museum
where by great good luck there was a show of French
Impressionists from private collections. In the silence of
the museum rooms, she was at first lonely and a little
self-conscious, unable to concentrate, walked too rapidly
from one painting to another, not involved beyond tick-
ing off the painters, waiting for the moment when she
could see and be absorbed. Finally she sat down on a low
velvet couch and let everything subside. A bearded young
man went past, clearly doing what she could not do, stopping before a Monet of haystacks at sunset, walking away
from it, coming back. After he had gone on into the next
room, Anna slipped into the state of grace she had waited
for. She began to see that Monet painting, the astonishing
crimson on one side of the haystack catching the setting
sun, the strange light on the field surrounding it, light
caught at an instant of change, and held there forever. A
work of art that could happen like this for one pair of eyes
after another forever. Anna sat there for a long moment
in a prolonged state of vision, simply *seeing.* After that she
walked through the next room, acutely aware of a Pissaro
of a few houses along a country road, and finally again sat
down to take in a large Cezanne still life. Why did the
monumental white tablecloth and its blue fold at one corner create such sensational response? Finally she was delighted by a small Vuillard interior and decided that that
was the one she would like to steal and take home to Ned.

When they were first married Ned had taken her to the museum in Boston several times and they had played a game, separating for a half-hour or so, then leading each other to the painting they would like to steal and take home. Ned had often chosen Vuillard, of course she realized now because in those small records of bourgeois life in Paris, he felt at home. "It is intimacy," he had said once. "How few painters have ever communicated that!" "Bonnard maybe," she had suggested. "Oh yes, but in a far less subtle way." In those days they had enjoyed arguing things out. Now any difference of opinion seemed like an assault. And perhaps was used as an assault.

Ned's shadow had followed her to the museum, and Anna left.

Chapter IX

Ned, feeling peaceful, was reading the paper with Fonzi at his feet. Just as well that Anna would not be home for another night, he thought. He would have a game of court tennis with Johnny and dine at the club. It felt like a reprieve. And just as Anna was thinking about the program for her concert, he was cogitating a rather radical change at the bank. The very high interest rates were becoming a real problem, but he had an idea about short-term investments and he was eager to talk it over with his colleagues. It was nearly nine and he intended to walk to the office, but first he would get the mail. How amazing to open the box and take out a fat envelope from the Pittsburgh hotel! He turned it over in his hands, then decided to go back to the apartment and read it before taking Fonzi for a short walk.

"Yes, Fonzi, in a minute," he said, as the little dog barked and ran around the room in a frenzy of expectation. "Lie down," Ned said firmly, as he slid a thin letter opener under the flap and neatly opened the letter, as though it were some sort of official document. He had had very few letters from Anna, and those few were usually full of exclamations and written in a large flowing hand. This one covered two pages on both sides and was written with care. "Oh dear," he murmured, full of dread. "If only

Anna would be silent," he said to Fonzi. "Only three days and she has to write me a small essay, it would seem."

At first what he read he had heard many times before . . . a defense of her anger. But when he came to what she said about love-making, Ned felt the blood rising to his head and his only need was to black out on it, not know that it had been said. He tore the letter into small pieces and threw it down the chute. There! "That's torn it, Fonzi," he said. Never never would he expose himself again. He would pretend that he hadn't read the letter. He was so angry that all he could feel was a need for violence, for some wild offensive act. He paced up and down, while Fonzi followed him with frightened eyes. "Come on, we'll go for a walk. Don't cower like that. I'm not angry with you," but the tone was angry and Fonzi followed him on the leash with his tail between his legs.

She had called him an angry man and she was damned right. People shouldn't ever talk about such things. It was . . . it was—Ned hunted for words as he walked fast, hardly waiting for Fonzi to do his business, he was so driven— invasion of privacy. Destructive. So that was what was going on in her head while she lay there, crying out in what he had presumed was ecstasy! How could he ever see her again? Sit across the table at breakfast from a woman who had stripped him down to the marrow? I didn't deserve this, Ned thought, filled with self-pity, and what's more I'm not going to take it lying down. Divorce? And have her tell a lawyer all about it? No, they would have to live along side by side in enmity forever. What- ever Ned did that day he did in a black fog. And the only release was a punishing game that evening which he lost because he went at it in a fury.

"Hey," Johnny said after they had showered and were having a coke at the bar. "The joker's wild today . . . what got into you anyway? You were out for blood!"

"Not your blood, Johnny!"

"You scared me."

"Did I?" Ned laughed, but it came out more like a sob. "Not enough to keep you from winning anyway. And I wanted to win."

"Whatever it was that made you so mad, you played a fierce, fast game, old boy. I tell you," Johnny wiped his glasses and put them on again, "you were pretty formidable."

"But you won." Ned knew it was childish to mind as much as he did, but he did mind.

"It seemed as though you wanted to beat the wall down! I mean . . . beyond the game . . . your ball went wild. That's what scared the shit out of me."

Ned shook his head as though to shake obsession off. "Well," he said after swallowing half the glass of coke. "It just goes to show that anger may rev up the motor but then overcharges it, I guess. You can't win that way."

Ned blinked and looked at Johnny for the first time, that plain open face, sandy hair, not a mean thought in the old boy with whom he had played football at Exeter, and smiled a sheepish smile. Exhaustion had crept in now.

"You were awfully mad at something—that's for sure."

They had known each other for years. Ned liked being with Johnny because Johnny was so easygoing, easy with himself, one of the few men Ned ever saw who was not ridden by ambition. He had done reasonably well as a corporation lawyer in his father's firm, had married happily and had three children, a pair of twins and an older daughter.

"Don't you ever get mad at anything, Johnny? Don't you ever want to break down a wall?"

"Of course I do. I don't know what this is all about, Ned, but I'm kind of glad you can get that het up. You're such a controlled person, you know, it makes you more human. Sally says I have a terrible temper, if you must know."

"Really? I thought you two were like a Philippina in an almond, two in one.

"We are, I guess. But that doesn't mean we never fight."

"Doesn't it?"

"Come on, Ned, you weren't born yesterday. There's some anger in any close relationship. Sometimes I think that's healthy. It clears the air, Hey, don't look at me as though I were crazy! I mean it."

Ned twisted the glass round and round on the counter as though it were a mathematical equation. "I was brought up to regard anger as a sin, for which one paid a very high price afterward in guilt. I hate it. For me anger is a poison. I can't see it as healthy whatever you say, Johnny."

"O.K., then maybe you worked out some of the poison today."

Ned shook his head and was silent. He just couldn't talk to anybody about Anna. Not even good old Johnny who, he was quite aware, had opened the door for him to do so.

"See you next week, Johnny. I'd better be getting along. Fonzi will be waiting for his walk."

"Anna not home?"

"Oh, she's in Pittsburgh . . . "

"Well, so long, old boy. Good luck!"

After Johnny left, Ned sat on for a few minutes, too tired suddenly to move. Anger "healthy"? He felt sick.

Chapter X

Anna got home early in the afternoon, to be welcomed by an ecstatic Fonzi and an otherwise silent and empty apartment. She had half hoped that Ned might have left a note for her, a welcome home, or even perhaps an answer to her letter, but she found nothing to acknowledge her existence. There were no flowers, she noted, wishing she had brought the pink roses from the hotel. Well, that at least could be remedied. She changed into comfortable clothes and went out into the bright October afternoon with Fonzi, walked down Charles Street to the florist on the corner and chose twelve enormous African daisies in every shade of deep rose, orange, yellow, and red, then added in a few sprays of eucalyptus. In her mood of expectation and dread, they gave a note of triumph, a kind of homage even to Ned—yes, homage, she thought, rather surprised at the word she had conjured up. She was terribly anxious now to see him, to run a finger along his stern mouth, to tell him that after all she was still very much in love. For her something had been solved, at least temporarily, by saying what she felt in the letter. Having said it, it was no longer a poison, the anger inside her. She could lay it all aside.

And in this mood she read the mail, finding in it two

letters from Pittsburgh, one from the woman who had
sent the flowers. "You are quite marvelous," it said, "I
wonder whether you know how transcendant you are,
how your singing does more than fill our ears with beauty,
but lifts us up beyond petty cares into what life is really
all about."

Anna set it down on the table beside her and leaned
back in her chair. When people said things like that they
never seemed quite believable. Could it be true, she wondered? And if so why was it that in her life itself she could
never achieve this, never transcend? Never be as Ned's
wife what she had been for him when he did not know
her?

The other was a short note in purple ink from Sophie,
"I wanted to say goodbye, but was afraid to wake you. I
took an early plane to the coast. What fun we had! You are
quite adorable, etc. Love, Sophie." The "etc." was so characteristic it made Anna smile. Yes, she thought, we did
have fun, glorious fun.

"Life is good, Fonzi. Come and let me scratch your
tummy," and she lifted Fonzi up for a little nuzzle. It
seemed an eternity until five-thirty when she could expect Ned to come home.

At half past five she was dressed in a gray dress that she
had worn only once before on an occasion she remembered as happy. Anna was superstitious enough to accord
dresses a genius of their own, so much so that she had
sometimes laid aside forever a dress associated with pain
or disaster, and she realized "disaster" was often caused
by anger, an inappropriate outburst on a social occasion.
Am I really an impossible human being, she asked herself,
standing in front of the long mirror in the bedroom? What
she saw with her eyes was a poised, handsome woman
who could not help but draw attention, who had an air
about her which was almost beauty, but not quite. Not
quite because it was less stylized than true beauty, too

mobile, she thought, smiling at herself. What her eyes saw made her smile, what her mind said to her was not flattering.

There you are, her mind said, with everything in your favor, including a real gift as a performer, and then you wreck it all, like a bad spoiled child.

No, Anna protested, spirit or whatever it was, against reason, not a bad child. A child who can't keep anything back, for whom life is so close to the surface that there is no defense, no armor, a child so hungry for love and praise that a cold word can throw her off balance.

At that moment, she heard Ned's key in the lock and ran to the door.

"Darling!" she cried out, "At last you're here!"

"More or less here," Ned said after kissing her on the cheek and moving past her to hang up his overcoat and to greet Fonzi who was barking in great excitement. In that second of his turning away, Anna's state of mind changed. What had made her imagine that Ned would take her in his arms? That he would show some joy?

"Well," he said, "I've a table at the club for seven." He looked at his watch. "There's time for a drink before I change. Scotch all right?"

"Of course." No champagne for her this time, she noted.

"Your mother said the concert went well. I was glad to hear that," Ned said from the kitchen, so Anna could not see his face. He brought in the drinks, set hers down by the sofa, taking his over to his chair where he could put his feet up. "And what did you do with your day alone in Pittsburgh?"

"I went to the museum and saw a lovely show of Impressionists from private collections—what a treat! There was one of those Monet haystacks in evening light . . . and an exquisite Vuillard I wanted to steal for you." The hungry-for-love-and-praise child told the bad, spoiled child to keep it cool. If he was not going to give, neither would she, Anna decided, as he had not reacted to her offering, her reference to the game they had played long ago. "And what have you been doing with yourself?"

"Working hard. Things are awfully uneasy these days in the financial world. The market is nervous . . . and so am I, I suppose. The banks are in an awful squeeze and will be, I expect until the interest rates go down."

Anna sat very still, sipped her drink, and waited.

"Oh, I played a fast game of court tennis with Johnny and he won. I walked Fonzi, of course. He wanted to attack a Great Dane!" Hearing his name, Fonzi, who was lying at Ned's feet, looked up and gave a short bark. "Yes, you did, Fonzi." Ned was smiling now, but not at her, Anna knew. And with every minute, the gulf between them was widening.

"Oh, Nancy came backstage."

"Nancy who?"

"Nancy Furman . . . we were at Juilliard together. She had quite a fine soprano voice, but she gave it all up when she married, and now has four children."

"And no regrets?"

"Maybe some regrets—I guess she sort of envied me. But one can't have everything."

"And you didn't envy her, of course." Ned was looking across at her for the first time, but the look was faintly hostile.

Anna reacted, she couldn't help it. "A lot of women have four children or six or eight children, you know. But very few indeed have a voice like mine. Oh, Ned," she said, taking her drink over to the windows and looking out over the lights of the Common, "I wish you could have heard the duet with Sophie, it was so beautiful, such a release, somehow transcendant."

"And the reviews?"

"Good."

"You've come home on the crest of the wave, I see."

"Anna Lindstrom is on the crest of the wave . . . in

Pittsburgh I planned out the whole Dallas concert. I'm going to sing the *Kindertoten Lieder*." Anna was suddenly afraid Ned would needle her about that, singing the death of children she did not want to have, so she went on quickly, "Anna Fraser wonders if you got her letter." There, it was out!

"Yes, I did," Ned got up. "I guess I'd better have a shower. Have a look at Chancellor and tell me what is happening when I come back."

Alone with the tv on, Anna burst into tears. Fonzi came trotting over, his tail wagging, eager to lick them. "Yes, Fonzi, darling, do lick my tears." And, well licked, Anna managed to stop crying. She knew it would only irritate Ned if he came back to find her, dissolved. "I despise your tears," he had said, this husband, this mortal enemy. And now she despised them herself. They were the other side of rage, as irrational as rage. And in the hour since Ned's arrival, rage was eating into her again like a poison she could not handle.

On the screen a short section about havens for abused wives was going on. Under the Reagan cuts these havens, which only recently had been a concern of government, were in danger of closing. Anna's attention was riveted on this problem when Ned came back, looking elegant in a dark blue suit, cool, contained, and, she had to admit, extremely distinguished.

"Is this very distinguished man really taking me to dinner?"

"Yes, this poor worm is really taking the diva to dinner!"

"Oh, Ned," Anna stood up, laughing. It was so easy to forget the bitterness if he gave even a little. "Come on, let's go then."

"You be a good dog, Fonzi, and we'll have a walk when we get back." Fonzi went to his bed and curled up.

And Ned and Anna walked down to the Somerset Club, arm in arm.

When they had settled at their usual table in a corner

and had ordered, Ned looked up and asked "What was all that about shelters for battered women on the news?"

"It looks as though the cuts would mean some of them at least would have to close."

"A bad business, I'm afraid."

"Just when a start had been made, it seems too cruel, cruel and stupid, to cut off help . . . " Here Anna felt safe with Ned. About such matters he was generous, and occasionally put her to shame by his awareness and her own ignorance. He was on so many charitable committees. "Ned, do you think the private sector can take over all that the government is cutting out? What does it really mean? Will those women again have nowhere to take refuge? I mean, how can we go back on so many promises?"

"You've asked a lot of questions and I'm afraid I don't have any answers. Can the private sector fill the gap? I guess I must be asked that question a dozen times a day. You can have no idea what the demands are right now. My secretary spends about half her time trying to reassure scared people, people who are involved in valuable work and scared to death that they won't be able to carry on. The foundations are in all this up to their ears."

"I read somewhere that Reagan gives one percent of his income to charity . . . one percent, Ned!"

At this Ned smiled, "It's a free country, Anna, after all."

"It's disgusting."

"It is his business, not ours. Our business, as I see it, is to manage to give here and there a great deal more than we have done—but then how does one choose?"

They had this evening found a subject they could talk about and plunged into it with zest because it was, or seemed, safe.

"You're so generous, it makes me feel ashamed."

"Nonsense, there is a fairly wide margin. It's not really generous to give what you have. Generosity, as I see it, is giving what you don't have."

"It sounds simple, but it isn't. But I guess it is something ingrained in the ethos here, isn't it?"

"The old Puritan ethic of self-mortification, you mean?"

"In your world, the people we know in this room, for example, institutional giving is as taken for granted as brushing one's teeth is my guess . . . and not just for tax purposes either. Hospitals, symphony orchestras, colleges and universities—oh Ned, does anything really important ever pay its way?"

"I never thought about it."

"The arts appear always to be the orphan children of a civilization. It doesn't seem right somehow. The enormous power money has to support or not to support. . . . It's a little scary."

"You bet it is!"

"Someday will you tell me what things we—I mean you and I—are supporting? I really don't know." It was true. One thing Ned and she had never approached as a mutual problem or responsibility was money. From the beginning it had not been discussed between them. Ned paid the bills and had never questioned any of them. Anna paid for her clothes and whatever she wanted for herself out of what she earned. And she gave what she could to help people and causes that she felt to be her own concerns, a home for retired singers for one.

"I'll give you a list," Ned said, "if you will first tell me what you want for dessert. Strawberry mousse, for instance?"

Anna was smiling.

"What's amusing?"

"That we have fought about everything except money. I bet there are very few marriages where money has not been a thorn in the side. My father, for instance, never gave mother enough for the housekeeping expenses— that is what finally drove her into selling antiques."

"Money and sex were the two taboo subjects in that generation, I suppose. My mother, on the other hand, had the fortune, so she never suffered in that way."

"Was it a happy marriage, Ned?"

"God knows. The legend is that it was. How can I possibly know? I suspect that my father felt somewhat smothered, but that is only a guess."

"If sex and money were the taboos in that generation, what are the taboos in ours?" Anna was feeling happy and exhilarated. Maybe after all her letter was having an effect, for Ned seemed at ease with himself that evening.

"In ours?" he frowned. "Privacy. Holding anything back. It's the age of turning oneself inside out or be damned."

"Oh?" Anna raised an eyebrow. For there had been something fierce in the way he said it, and she changed the subject. Should they accept an invitation to dine out that weekend? It would mean staying in town.

"Let's go down to the country," Ned answered. "Fonzi deserves a little outing for a change."

"And so do we!"

But when they got home, while Ned was taking Fonzi for his evening walk and Anna got undressed with a Haydn concerto on the player, she knew that the dinner conversation had been a reprieve. Sooner or later they would have to talk about themselves.

When Ned came back, she was undressed and pulled him down to sit on the bed and kissed him on the mouth. "I do love you," she said.

"Even in the dark?" He was looking down, and he had not kissed her when she kissed him.

"Don't." Anna sat up.

"Don't what?"

"Don't shut me out."

"I'm not shutting you out. I just asked a civil question."

"You've read my letter. I am not going to repeat what I said."

"I'd better sleep on the sofa," Ned got up, but she caught his hand and pulled him back.

"We have to talk, Ned."

"I don't have anything to say." He would not look at her and Anna sat up, not angry but as cold as ice.

"Very well then, sleep on the sofa. This seems to be the beginning of the end."

Ned grabbed his pillow and pulled it out from under Anna's head quite roughly. But then, as though something held back, held down for years exploded in his head, and with a strange exhilarating fury, he turned back at the door. "I'm sick to death of the scenes and the needling. Your letter was an attack below the belt," and as Anna laughed at the unconscious accuracy of this, "What's funny about that? When I had read it I tore it up. I felt castrated if you must know. All those nights when you pretended to be in ecstasy came back, all those lies . . . "

"They weren't lies!"

"You act all the time. How am I ever to know when you are honest?"

"Ned!" Anna was not angry. She was too astonished, observing with a curious satisfaction that Ned was too angry to control himself.

"You want a confrontation. You have been trying to get me to answer your anger with anger. Very well. Your letter made me furious. I didn't deserve it. For two years I've tried to love you, Anna, but you cannot behave like a rational human being. It's gotten so I dread coming home. I dread to find you in a bad mood."

"I've had good reason to be depressed sometimes. You will never understand what it is to be as exposed as I am, to have to sit still under attacks in the newspapers, not able to defend myself."

"I think you are a little paranoid about reviews."

"Paranoid?" This word made Anna get out of bed and stand facing him, tears of rage pouring down her cheeks. "You beast! You prehistoric brute!"

Ned threw the pillow onto the bed. "What you need is

a psychiatrist, my dear. All these rages, all these tears seem to be close to psychotic."

"And what are your withdrawals, coldness, inability ever to say a loving word? Normal? You have the sympathetic nerve of a cobra!"

"And you, I suppose, are a great human being, open and loving—why not? All your friends are sycophants, Anna."

"What?" Anna pushed past Ned and paced up and down in the big room. He followed her, picking Fonzi up and holding the little dog in his arms.

"Don't scream. It upsets Fonzi!"

Anna sat down on the sofa, her head in her hands. Ned set the dog down and stood in the window looking out on the Common.

"I'll go to a psychiatrist if you will come with me," Anna said, after a pause.

"You think I need help, as they say? Come now!"

"You don't have the guts to do it."

"It would be an invasion of my privacy. If that is cowardice, not to want to unbutton everything secret and private to a perfect stranger, have it your way! I regard psychiatry as self-indulgence."

"Unless the person is mad like me?"

"If a total lack of self-control is a kind of madness, yes. You might learn something about these angers that destroy anyone who comes anywhere near you. You might learn the virtue of restraint."

The last word was said so fiercely that Anna suddenly burst into laughter. In spite of Ned's attacks in the last minutes, she felt a kind of relief, even exhilaration. She saw Ned's look of amazement at her laughter.

"Can't you see that this fight, however painful it is, is a lot healthier than all the silences of the last months? At last you are letting your anger out."

"That's what you wanted, isn't it?" Ned flung himself down in his chair.

"Yes, I did," Anna said in a calm voice.

"So you think you've won. And the next thing will be to get me to cry, I suppose." He put his head in his hands, then after a moment he said, "I can't see that bad behavior is ever good. You appear to enjoy being angry. It just makes me feel rotten, ashamed!" He lifted his head and looked at her, "And I hate you for making it happen, if you must know."

"But I love you for letting it happen."

"Love? In this context? Love? You don't know what it means."

"What does it mean then?"

"Restraint."

"I would say giving." Again Anna was walking up and down thinking aloud, thinking with her whole body, "That's the crux of it for me. Opening oneself, one's deepest self to the stranger, growing out of the prehistoric era of blind passion into a human place, a million years down the road, toward some kind of communion. Love is not shutting out buried parts of the self. It is allowing them to exist, facing them with a lover."

"You've had enough of those, you ought to know."

"At least I gave to the people I loved. I didn't hold back." Ned had never shown any jealousy before about the past and when they were first in love they had each talked quite a lot about their experiences.

"How could you—with so many?"

"Don't jeer," she said coldly. "It really is not appropriate."

"Well, you were pretty promiscuous."

At this Anna got up and rushed at him, hitting him on the back with her fists. "I was never promiscuous, you filthy liar!"

"Get away from me, Anna. Don't touch me!" He turned and pushed her away quite roughly. "I find this violence sickening."

"It's healthy!" she shouted. "You can't stand anyone even your wife coming close to you!"

"Hitting someone is not coming close, Anna." Ned's face was white.

Anna flung herself down on the sofa and sat there hugging his pillow. Then, seeing Fonzi's stricken look where he lay in his bed, she burst into tears.

And following her eyes, Ned shouted, "Now you have made Fonzi miserable! All you ever think about is your feelings—you are the most selfish person I've ever known!"

"*I* have made him miserable!" Anna, hugging the pillow, rocked back and forth. "Ned," she said quietly, "the only real emotion I have ever seen you express is anger. Are you aware that deep feeling, at least the only deep feeling you ever show is *anger?* Have you ever been honest enough with yourself to find out why that is? It isn't normal, you know. Why can't you show tenderness? Why can't you ever express love? You're sick." And she laughed her theatrical laugh. "When are you going to develop to the point of giving up fur for skin, you stupid prehistoric animal?"

"Ha," Ned mimicked her laugh. "My God, what an actress you are! Can't you ever stop acting, Anna, even in bed?"

Anna looked up and suddenly threw the pillow at him with all the force she could muster sitting down. Ned caught it, looked as though he would throw it back, but instead laid it down carefully on the chair.

"You wanted to throw it," Anna said, laughing again, "Why couldn't you? You couldn't because you censor any natural impulse you may have. What you can't understand is that what you call acting is simply doing what I feel, being whatever I am at the moment to the fullest possible extent."

"Maybe, but if everyone did exactly what he or she felt

at any given moment, we would be in a state of perpetual war and society would have a complete breakdown. I can't see that anarchy in personal relations or anywhere else is any solution."

"No, you can't see very much or very far when it comes to loving, can you, Ned?"

"I can see far enough to know that a scene like this is purely negative in its effect, Anna. That I can see with extreme clarity. The whole apartment is infected. You call that healthy! Good Christ!" He flung himself down in his chair.

Anna closed her eyes. Where words had been crashing around, the silence was now even louder. Had they reached the end? Was there nothing possible now except to go in opposite directions as fast as they could go and lick their wounds?

"When you were away I managed to get back to normal for three or four days," Ned said calmly. "Then that letter came."

"It was a gift from my deepest self to yours," Anna said. What was there to lose now? She would pack a bag in a little while and go to her mother's.

"Pearls before swine," Ned smiled an ironic smile.

"Do you think you could listen to me for a moment, stop being defensive for a moment?" Anna said gently. "Why is the only feeling you allow yourself anger? Please try to tell me, Ned. Then I'll go to mother's, if that's what you want, and leave you to find your own peace. Please, Ned, try to tell me."

"Anything else is too dangerous." Ned looked across at her and what Anna saw was so much pain that she dropped her eyes. She recognized the truth of what he had said, and she knew how hard it had been for him to go even that far with his own secretive self. But if there never had been trust, how could there have been love?

"No love then," she murmured, "no love, no love."

"Love, Anna, but not your kind."

"We're married but we're not kin."

"It would be incest if we were, wouldn't it?"

"At this point can we do without cleverness? That, if you must know, is acting too. Evading. Hiding."

"Yes, Professor Lindstrom. I'm listening. What is the next lesson?"

Anna was beyond being hurt or even angry. "Sometimes I feel so deprived because I can never give you my best gifts . . . I can't even give you my love because you can't take it. It is not acceptable. Can't you see that that makes for desolation and despair?"

"I don't measure up." Anna watched him rub his eyes, as though rubbing something away, and was silent.

But, as he said nothing she finally said, "It's not a question of measuring up, whatever that means."

"What is it a question of?"

"Giving—giving just a little—"

"I can't."

"Why can't you? It's so strange," and Anna heard her voice rising. "If we can't understand each other . . . if we are poles apart . . . " she left it up in the air. "You show compassion for those abused women. You are really concerned about *them*, but you can't see that you have hurt me terribly and I need your compassion, Ned, I need it. I need your love." Ned stared at her, silent. "I can't live in this cold air. I can't sing when we are at odds."

"You did pretty well in Pittsburgh, nevertheless."

"Yes, because I was able to get through my own anger and pain to reach out to you, don't you see?"

"Reach out with a body blow? Come now, Anna."

"Oh, oh," Anna groaned. She felt her face crumpling up into an ugly grimace. She felt ugly, rejected, an orphan with no shelter. Tears, cramped, miserable tears stung her eyes. Then she looked across at Ned and asked in a quiet voice, "Ned, do you love me? Do you need me?"

There was a second's pause before Ned answered miserably, "I don't know."

"If you don't know, why did you marry me? Why?"

"Because I fell in love, Anna. But how could I know that I was marrying a fury? How could I possibly know?"

"Only an emotionally stupid person could have imagined that Anna Lindstrom had no temperament, had the surface of a still pond. For a highly intelligent man, you are apparently retarded where feelings are concerned—you behave like a spoiled child who wants what he wants but on his terms, who won't give or even try to understand!"

"And you who think you know everything about feeling—I begin to hate the word!—can't control yours. I have very little respect for lack of control. It is you who behave like a spoiled child, Anna!"

"At least I am honest, honest with myself and with you."

"Does honesty have to scream, does honesty have to weep, does honesty mean hitting somebody in the back? Stop and think, Anna—if you are capable of thinking!"

It shot through Anna's consciousness that they were now behaving like two dogs, barking at each other and what they actually said did not matter. It was the fight itself that mattered. She did not reason it out, but she sensed it and suddenly barked very loudly at him, "Woof! Woof! Woof!" she barked.

And Ned got up from his chair and barked back, "Woof! Woof! Woof yourself!"

It was too much for Fonzi who rose from bed and ran from one to the other barking his short sharp barks of excitement and pleasure. And at that second, they broke out of the maze and began to laugh hysterically. Ned laughed so much that he got out of breath and had to sit down, and Anna on the sofa was wiping her eyes.

"Oh Anna, you are marvelous!" was what he said when he had caught his breath.

"At last," she murmured, "at last." A year's tension and irritability had broken down and they were free of it . . . at least for now.

"Come on, let's go for a walk! Fonzi has had too much excitement and he must need to go out again . . . " and Ned went to the coatroom and came back with Anna's purple velvet and sable cloak.

"Darling, not that one! It's my best!"

"Why not your best? You have just given a superb performance—as a dog!" He was laughing at her now but there was no irony in it.

"Very well, my idiot husband, I'll wear it if it will make you happy! Just let me get into some slacks and a sweater."

A few minutes later they were walking slowly arm in arm across the Common and out onto Tremont Street, Fonzi's feet twinkling along ahead. The cold air felt delicious, and every now and then they stopped to look up at the sky.

"Too bad the lights are so bright . . . the stars must be wonderful in the country tonight."

"I can see Orion," Ned answered, "over there back of the Ritz!"

Anna longed to ask him whether he did not see now that anger let out was healthy, was better than contained irritability, but she told herself to be quiet. She had won this time, won by a fluke, and it was not the moment to rub it in. Besides she was tingling all over with the pleasure of feeling Ned's arm in hers, of being with him. It had been such a lonely state of affairs for so very long.

"Yes," she said, "I see Orion."

It was after midnight when they were finally in bed, and Anna, giving Ned a smile, turned out the light.

Chapter XI

In the morning they ate a huge breakfast of bacon and eggs which Ned insisted on getting. Anna, while she dressed, could hear him whistling an air from *Carmen* . . . of all things! It was just as always, Ned handing her the middle section of the *Times* while he turned to the business section. It was just as always, no word of any importance said. They discussed the day ahead, Anna off to her lesson at ten, Ned to the office, and a getaway to the country after five. Anna would make lasagna and a salad, Ned would stop at the bakery on Charles Street on the way home and pick up bread there and wine. They could shop for a roast or something on Saturday, "and go to that fresh vegetable place if it's still open." It was just as always, but now these mundane matters had taken on a kind of sheen. There was an air of happiness, of intimacy about it all. And when Anna said, as Ned prepared to leave, his brief case in his hand, "I do love you," and Ned's only response was "good" she kissed him and did not mind that even after last night he could not say more.

For once, we are safe, she thought as she took the breakfast dishes out to the kitchen, rinsed them, and put them in the dishwasher. But would it, could it last? Was this only a truce or was it, perhaps, after two years, a new begin-

ning? Ned had yielded nothing, had not said a loving word
in the night. Why didn't she mind? She had woken up
with him curled around her, his legs wound around hers,
his hand folded around her breast. The sweetness of it!
She told herself that if they could get through the weekend in this tender mood, then perhaps the new beginning
would seem real.

She called Teresa. "I think things are going to be better.
We had an awful fight, the worst ever last night."

Teresa laughed.

"I know it sounds crazy, Mama, but Ned had to let his
anger out. It was poisoning him."

"I never cease to marvel at your idea of what is good—
a terrible fight apparently is."

"It ended with laughter, Mama—that was what was
good." But Anna didn't tell her mother that they had
barked like dogs. It seemed now as secret as describing a
sexual act might have been.

"Well, bravo! At any rate you sound happy for a
change."

"I'm dying to get to work on the Dallas concert. It is
going to be a difficult program—Mahler, Fauré and
Brahms. I've got to stretch my range a bit, but I think I
can do it. Hard work for the next two weeks."

"Well, that's your element. Good luck. And have a
happy weekend—I presume you are off to the country?"

"And what are you going to do?

"Putter around the house, do some cooking. Susan and
Elizabeth are coming for dinner on Sunday. I may go for
a walk. It's a beautiful day."

"Ciao, darling."

What would happen, Anna asked herself, if I became an
easygoing, never angry, socially impeccable person with

never a violent word or mood to shatter the amenities? Would Ned like that? I can't believe he would! But then would she like it if Ned screamed at her and burst into tears? She had to admit the answer was yes. Anger expressed had some life in it, whereas coldness and withdrawal shut life out. Ned was so afraid of violence, so outraged by anger because they threatened to crack him open. Anna felt very much alive when she was angry. It was a costly business though because afterward came remorse and, in relation to Ned, a sense of inferiority. That she could not deny. The world in general would be on his side, but was the world always right?

It was clear to her in the brilliant sunlight of that morning that neither of them was going to change. What then? And why do people in love want to change each other? What is the war really all about? If we could only go deeper, only get to *that,* to talking about *that!*

But she had seen something in Ned she had never seen until last night and that was the pain, the vulnerability when he said that showing feeling was too dangerous. She had for a second seen so much pain in his eyes that she had had to lower hers.

It was time to walk Fonzi if she was not to be late for her lesson, but she simply had to find a passage in Rilke's letters that she had marked some time ago . . . where was the book? She searched in the bookcases, with no luck, and finally went off with Fonzi, trying to remember exactly what it was—and then it was there. It sprang up before her as she had read it on the left side of a page, near the bottom, "Perhaps everything terrible in us is at its deepest being something helpless that wants help from us." Or was it, "deepest level"? Walking Fonzi in the jubilant autumn sunlight, past the flowing beds of chrysanthemums, and a jay screaming in a dogwood tree, Anna thought about this phrase that haunted her.

"What is the terrible thing in me that needs help?" she

wondered. "What is the terrible thing in Ned that keeps him separated out into compartments? Shall we ever know? Can love do it?"

"Fonzi," she asked aloud, "he said I was the most selfish person he had ever known? Can that be true?" Fonzi responded by barking and pulling her on.

"Soon you can run free, my little dog! But try to take it easy now." And the obedient Fonzi trotted along, his nose to the ground, telling her with an occasional growl or bark that a squirrel or a Great Dane perhaps had passed by. Fonzi's soul appeared to be in his nose and his tongue. And where, she wondered, is ours? Perhaps where feeling and thinking come together. Well, Anna thought, I am certainly feeling alive this morning! Happiness like this was so rare and so poignant that she felt tears pricking her eyes.

For once they were going to the country in a mood of happy expectancy, so it did not even seem too hard that Mrs. Fraser was at her house next door and wanted them for Sunday lunch.

"We'll have Saturday anyway, plant bulbs, maybe have a walk on the beach with Fonzi—now at last it's October and we can let him off the leash." Fonzi, sitting between them in the car, wagged his tail. Ned, driving through the Friday traffic, was silent. But Anna felt his silence as companionable. She was at peace.

She was willing to follow Ned's mood, not to try to talk seriously, just to be. They ended that good day in bed making love and laughing. What made them laugh was Fonzi's anxiety to get into the act and refusal to stay at the bottom of the bed. "Oh, you foolish little dog . . . " Anna reached out and stroked his ears.

"It's hard to be a dog," Ned said. "He wants so much to

be included. Here Fonzi, you can lie on my chest!" But
Fonzi, entranced, had to lick Ned's throat and mouth a
little too thoroughly for comfort and finally had to be
forced back to his usual place where he was delighted to
find Anna's bare foot to lick. "Ah," Ned sighed, and
reached over to take Anna's hand and lie there, then,
beside her in the dark, hand in hand, until they fell asleep.

When Anna woke and looked out through the crimson
leaves of a maple to a blue, blue sky she jumped out of
bed. "Let's walk first!" Anna said at the window, breathing in the sharp morning air and shivering.

"We have to plant 100 bulbs," Ned answered, yawning.

"No," Anna turned and blew him a kiss. "Let's not
work, I feel like a walk. It's low tide. I can smell the salt
and seaweed from here."

"Very well. If you will make blueberry pancakes first.
It was rather an athletic night and I'm starving," he said,
smiling his secret smile.

"Athletic! What a typical word!" And Anna disappeared
into the bathroom.

It took Ned quite a while to pull himself together.
Clearly he felt so unknotted, so relaxed that he didn't
really want to get up and lay there quite a while. When
he went down finally the pancakes were ready.

"Hurry up, you lazy man! The first batch is waiting for
you!"

"Yum!"

The breakfast room was filled with sunlight, sun dap-
pling the blue and white china and the bunch of fading
chrysanthemums from the last time.

"Ned, go and pick some fresh flowers . . . it's too beautiful here for those poor things!"

"Pancakes first. Then flowers," he said, taking the vase
off the table and throwing the flowers into the wastebas-
ket.

"I love this house," Anna said when they had settled

down and were drinking a second cup of coffee and waiting for the second batch. "It's so warm . . . even on a cold
October morning. How marvelous to have the whole day
here, alone!"

"Fonzi hasn't had his pancake," Ned said. "I'll get it."
When he came back he looked across at Anna who caught
his look and felt observed.

"What's on your mind?"

"Oh, I was just wondering why it made you so happy
when I said all those awful things?"

"You said I was marvelous!"

"Because in the midst of such a storm you made me
laugh, made us laugh!"

"Yes," Anna said, smiling, "it was rather wonderful."
Then she looked back at him, a long hard look. "I was
happy because at last you let the storm *out* . . . can't you
understand? I don't suppose I'll forget some of those ugly
things, but at least they're not buried inside you."

"Unburying is not necessarily exorcizing."

"No, but you do feel better, don't you?"

"Do I?"

"Oh, Ned!"

"Well," he gave a little cough, "I have to admit that I
do."

"Hurrah! Then let's go for a walk . . . "

"Come on, Fonzi!"

"I have to dress, but I won't be a minute."

So Ned went out into the wet grass with Fonzi to pick
a few late asters and chrysanthemums, and Anna ran upstairs. But, pulling on a turtleneck sweater, she realized
that he was right about exorcizing. The glorious fight had
left its detritus. And this she would have to deal with in
any way she could. "My friends are not sycophants," she
whispered. "Damn it!"

But out on the beach, walking fast, while Fonzi chased
gulls and picked up long pieces of seaweed and tossed

them around, the sheer space and light, and the long waves coming in gently and shirring into foam, Anna felt that nothing mattered very much, except the hour, the exhilaration, the sharp October air.

"It's the dark blue sea again . . . October," she murmured.

"A little bit of all right, eh?" Ned enjoyed using such expressions just to tease her.

"Nothing seems to matter on a day like this."

"Even the war between the Frasers?"

Anna stopped for a moment and leaned down to pick up a broken sand dollar. "Too bad it's broken . . . " Then she stood for a moment looking out to sea, to the dark line at the horizon. "I know it will sound crazy because outdoors like this the beauty is so immense and tranquil nothing seems to matter, but I think that way down deep, personal relations may have in them the roots of war and peace. I don't know how to say this . . . but, Ned, there's so much anger and frustration everywhere. I think every time two people achieve communion, it helps."

"Do you really?" Ned was interested and sceptical. "Why?"

"Because we are all members of each other."

"Tell that to a black in the ghetto!"

"He would say it doesn't look as if we believed that, but that doesn't mean I'm wrong. Ned, the deeper we go the more we are joined to everyone else . . . " but then she looked up and caught his expression of amused contempt. Contempt?

What he said was, "I can't follow your metaphysical flights, Anna." He gave her a piercing look. "Do you think we have achieved communion as you call it? Is that what screaming at each other does?"

"Oh no, we haven't achieved anything yet," Anna said passionately. "But can't you see, we can talk now and we haven't been able to talk for over a year!"

"Come on, Anna, let's run!" And Ned ran away with

Fonzi, ears flapping in the wind, after him. Anna walked down to the edge of the waves alone.

After a mile or so, Ned turned back. "Come on, Fonzi, we'd better go back. We don't want her to be cross, not on a day like this." He had enjoyed running, enjoyed the strength of his physical being, enjoyed getting a little out of breath. He could see that Anna was sitting now, looking out, her head in her hands. But he was not about to yield to a meditative mood, and when he and Fonzi got back to her, he said, "Come on, lazybones, we've got work to do," and he pulled Anna up. "Wow," he said, "you're a heavyweight, my fair lady!"

"I guess I am," Anna answered brushing the sand off. Sometimes she wished she could be as light as air and stop thinking . . . but she couldn't and so she was wondering whether she was indeed a heavyweight for Ned to bear through all the tensions and anguish of their marriage, and she asked herself once more whether it was mostly her own fault, conflicted as she was and, she supposed, always would be.

"Poor Fonzi," she said, "he's panting terribly . . . "

"Good for him," Ned said, leaning down to give the dog a pat. "He doesn't get enough exercise—and neither do I."

"But you have very long legs and he has very short ones."

"He can run like the wind, though, on those short legs! He'll sleep all day while we are planting bulbs . . . for it's got to be done, Anna, you know."

Done it was, for the rest of the morning, but after a short lunch of fruit and cheese, Anna pleaded for a rest and went upstairs to make the bed and then lie down on it while Ned went back to the garden with Fonzi. She must have fallen asleep, and when she woke thought she was dreaming for she heard Ferrier's voice singing the *Kindertoten lieder* . . . sat up, saw that the clock said four and ran downstairs, standing by the record player unable to decide whether to hear it through or take the record off. The poignance of that voice! Would she ever learn that ease, that perfect control, that depth? She stayed where she was, listening. She could handle the low notes, but that great crescendo in the upper register? It shouldn't be difficult, but it was. Oh, it was! Even Ferrier's voice showed the strain for a second. Anna was so concentrated that she didn't hear Ned behind her, took the record off and turned to find him there, grinning.

"Why did you do that?"

"You're going to sing it in Dallas, aren't you?"

"Yes." Anna was trembling. It was like an attack.

"Well then? I thought you might like to hear it. Ferrier is rather marvelous, isn't she?"

"You did it on purpose! Gave me the perfect rendition like a slap in the face . . . it's not fair!"

"I did it to wake you. It's nearly four, Anna." It had not occurred to Ned that she would find it offensive. But of course I can't win, he thought bitterly. Now she will make a scene.

"Let us say that you are not exactly the soul of tact. I can't possibly match that . . . and you know I can't." But Anna had now to hear the other side and turned the record over and went and sat down on the sofa. "Come and sit beside me Ned, I need you."

He sat down awkwardly beside her then, and they listened. Whatever else they could not share, Ned was thinking, they could share music. It was indeed a haunting sequence of songs. He slipped a hand into hers.

When it was over, they were silent. Ned knew that he ought to say something. He ought to say that of course Anna could sing this magnificently, that he knew she could. It was on the tip of his tongue, but somehow he couldn't utter the necessary words. A donkey in him, a stubborn donkey, balked.

And Anna reacted not with anger, but by moving away.

This battle was with herself. And as it sometimes did, what might have been anger turned into exaggerated self-justification. "You may not think so, but I can do it as well as she did. I have the instrument, Ned. And I have a great teacher."

"What more can you ask?"

"A word of reassurance from you," she flashed back. "I could do with some outdoor work. Any bulbs left?"

The moment of danger was past.

"I'm sorry if I did the wrong thing," Ned said then.

"Never mind, let's work first—and then," Anna said unexpectedly, "if you feel like accompanying me I'd like to sing. Oh, something easy and fun!"

"I'd like that," Ned said. Anna was rarely in the mood to sing at home, but occasionally they did play together when she could lay aside her professional self and all its anxieties and sing for pleasure. In college Ned had worked hard at the piano and had been quite surprised to find that he still had some skill. This had not happened for some time, this invitation to share music. He was pleased. So he was careful now to give Anna something easy to do so she would not get overtired and change her mind. They worked away in silence.

After a half-hour, Anna stretched and lay flat on her back for a moment, looking up through the leaves of the maple. "Look at the light . . . it's so beautiful," and then "Why is autumn, when everything is dying, so beautiful?"

"Not dying, going to sleep," Ned answered, brushing earth off his face. "Maybe you've had enough. I'll just get rid of this small bag of hyacinths and be with you."

"I'll put the roast in and have a shower."

"Good."

Anna stopped at the steps to the porch and looked back at Ned, kneeling in the grass, totally concentrated, and for a moment watched his deft hands, digging holes with his sharp trowel in a quick efficient rhythm. How could she not love this secret, ungiving, maddening man? In his own peculiar way he gave so much simply by being himself. The struggle with him was giving her a kind of life and self-knowledge she had never known until now. And maybe that was what it was all about.

Chapter XII

Mrs. Fraser did not relax her standards or change her way
of life in the country. She came down with Beulah, the
Nova Scotian cook who had been with her for over forty
years and was now rather crotchety, Maria, a West Indian
waitress and general help, and Maria's husband, Pedro,
who chauffeured the Mercedes and occasionally did some
odd jobs like bringing in wood though he was, as Maria
herself often said, "the laziest man God ever made."

It was hard these days for Pauline Fraser to come down
and face the garden, neglected since the old gardener had
died, and hard not to complain too much to Joe, a local
gardener who was apt to make egregious mistakes like
cutting off the asters in bud, thinking they were in seed.

"I know you can't help it, Joe, but you are giving me a
lot of pain in my old age."

"Sorry, Ma'am. It won't happen again."

"But something else will, Joe. Never mind," Mrs. Fraser
added quickly, for she was afraid Joe would walk off some
day. Workmen had pride these days but no standards.
And to Pauline Fraser, life had seemed for a long time a
matter of dealing with small disappointments and frustra-
tions as best she could.

That Sunday morning in honor of her luncheon guests
she decided to wear a blue and white silk dress in spite of

the chill in the air, threw a sweater on after breakfast and went out in rubber boots to pick a few late roses. There was mildew on some of the bushes . . . nothing to be done about that, she supposed. She cut and held up a yellow rose to smell its delicious slightly spicy scent and soon had quite an array of bloom in her basket.

Inside she took one look at Beulah, standing at the kitchen counter beating up egg whites for the lemon meringue pie, and fled to the pantry to arrange the roses. But of course the silverbowl she wanted was tarnished. Maria rarely noticed such things, so Mrs. Fraser got out the cleaning rag and polish and did it herself. And in the end, the centerpiece was really quite lovely, she thought.

Anna and Ned did not come over often, so Mrs. Fraser felt a little excited, if not exactly happy. She remained ill at ease with her daughter-in-law, who seemed a little larger than life, somehow. And she did occasionally wonder how Ned was faring as though, she smiled to herself, he had a tigress on his leash. No doubt the tigress occasionally purred, but Pauline Fraser suspected that she also roared. What an odd marriage it was! Ned was such a self-contained, self-assured man—except for his passion for music, and of course that was what explained it all. He had married music! That, Pauline Fraser, supposed, must have taken a certain audacity. And perhaps, she ruminated, a surprising self-abnegation. Ned could be quite ruthless. Heaven knows she had experienced that often enough. But then she had little loving kindness from her sons. She was kept at a distance. Their attitude was that she had let them down in some way after Angus died. They had never understood what it had been like for her to have her life cut in two, to be left stranded forever on an island of loss and pain.

"But I mustn't get teary this morning," she said to herself, and went upstairs to brief Maria on the table setting and to be sure she remembered to dust the glass tables on

the porch. By the time the sun was high, it would be warm
enough out there.

"I feel so old, Maria," she said after their little talk.
"Look at my face, a mass of wrinkles! I feel a hundred."

"You're only seventy, Ma'am, that's not old."

"It's awfully old," Pauline Fraser felt suddenly cross, "I
lost my husband thirty years ago . . . thirty years without
anyone."

"Now you keep those blues away," Maria said firmly.
"You look so pretty in that dress, and your son's coming
for dinner!" She plumped the bed pillows up just a little
impatiently. "Better keep away from Beulah, she's in a
bad mood."

"I know."

"High blood pressure," Maria said. "Some day she's
going to drop dead."

"No one seems to be very cheerful this morning," Pauline Fraser sniffed. "What a glum household this is!"

Maria refrained from comment. "I'd better get on with
it," she said. "There's a lot to do downstairs."

"Run along, Maria. You are no comfort this morning."

At the door, Anna let Ned go in alone and walked down
to the rose garden to smell the roses. She wanted to pick
one but didn't dare. No one ever picked in this garden
except Mrs. Fraser who was, it had to be faced, excruciatingly possessive about everything she owned. When Anna
came back toward the porch, Ned and his mother were
standing in the doorway and waved at her.

"Oh, those roses!" she called, "How do you ever do it?"

"So there's where you were!" Mrs. Fraser kissed her
daughter-in-law.

"I couldn't resist . . . "

"Well, sit down, Anna. What would you like to drink?

Sherry, Dubonnet? Ned, do the honors, please."

"Dubonnet is rather a treat."

"I'll have some myself. A treat?" Pauline Fraser smiled.
"I thought everyone drank Dubonnet these days. But of
course I don't move in your circles. It's champagne in
your circles, no doubt."

"We don't have a circle, Mama," Ned said, handing her
a glass and then taking Anna hers. "If you don't mind I'll
go and find the Scotch."

"Whatever does Ned mean about no circle?" Pauline
Fraser asked, as he disappeared.

"He's just teasing. But actually we don't go out much
anymore. Ned works awfully hard himself and I can't
have late nights when I'm getting ready for a concert."

"And you are now?"

"I go to Dallas in two weeks."

"Good heavens! Dallas? It seems so far away . . . "

"I'm in a panic, so let's talk about other things. This
room is such a pleasure," Anna said, "I love the flowery
cretonne. It's so summery and cheerful."

"They tell me wicker furniture is coming back. So after
forty years we are in fashion!"

And they talked on about nothing, like skaters on a
thinly iced-over pond. Anna was good at drawing Mrs.
Fraser out, about the garden, Beulah ("she appears to be
suffering from permanent menopause"), how Joe was
working out. Ned, nursing his Scotch, was silent, and
watched Anna's tactful treatment of his mother with a
certain amusement. At times she could act the perfect
lady with consummate skill, and he enjoyed watching her
do it. As for his mother, she looked suddenly old, her face
had become very wrinkled he noted, yet old age suited
her. It was more tolerable to see her at seventy spending
her life complaining than it had been when she was
younger.

And out of these thoughts Ned asked, "Who do you see
these days, Mama? How is Ernesta?"

"Oh, she's too busy to come and see me . . . she is on every imaginable committee and spends two days a week at the children's hospital. I'm lucky if she stops in once a month. Anne has cancer and refuses to see any of her old friends, at least refuses to see me. I seem to be some sort of leper. Sophia is a nervous wreck and ought to be in McLean."

Ned laughed, "Spare us the lugubrious list! Isn't anyone well and happy?"

"When you get to be my age, Ned, you'll understand. Old age itself is a kind of illness, you see." Pauline Fraser was sitting very erect and perhaps (at least Anna thought so) enjoying all this misery. It was her element.

"It's funny," Anna said, "but I have always looked forward to being old. I have known so many great old people —my teacher, Madama Protopova, is one. She is nearly eighty I believe, but she is still so vitally engaged in her life in and with music, still so fierce and demanding she acts like an electric current on her pupils. Old age can be a great time . . . I mean . . . "

"Well, if you have a career of course it's quite different," Pauline said, not pleased by the turn the conversation was taking. Why was it that Anna always managed to make her feel lacking in some way? "But if your life was cut in two when you were young, old age would only emphasize the loss."

Luckily Maria now made her appearance at the door. And they went into the dining room, an extremely formal room, daunting, Anna always felt, as though conversation died at its entrance.

"Oh, those roses!" she exclaimed as she unfolded her damask napkin. "Roses and silver, I had not thought of them as setting each other off, but they do! It's beautiful!"

"Mama is a genius at arranging flowers," Ned said, smiling across at his mother for the first time.

"Am I?" Pauline blushed with pleasure. "I've always enjoyed doing it."

Ned really should be kinder to his mother, Anna was thinking. It took so little, a compliment . . . why couldn't he do it more often?

"This soup is heaven," she said. "What is it? Cucumber?"

"I think so—it's a secret of Beulah's." Pauline was beginning to thaw. She felt less nervous, and so she turned to Anna and asked, "How do you two manage? About cooking, I mean?"

"Oh, we take turns . . . and then Felicia comes in every other day and makes a casserole and dessert."

"You have not made a cook out of Ned, have you?"

"Would that be a disaster?"

"No, a triumph, my dear!" Pauline Fraser was suffused with laughter. "When he was a boy he tried to make brownies and burned them. Another time, popovers that refused to rise—do you remember?" she asked Ned.

"Of course I remember. But you forget, Mama, that Paul and I lived in the little house for a summer, and we used to cook things."

Pauline finished her soup and the next course was served as she spoke in her forlorn voice, the voice that infuriated Ned. "I had a lot to bear that summer. Paul, you know," she said to Anna, "tried to commit suicide."

"That must have been awfully hard for you," Anna murmured.

"Yes, it was. Paul recovered. He had the help of a psychiatrist. He had someone to lean on. I had nobody and I never recovered."

"Must we dwell on the past, Mama? You are giving us a lovely meal. Let's enjoy it," Ned said coldly.

"Ned has no compassion," Pauline said to Anna. "You must have found that out by now."

"He can't show it," Anna said in the intimacy of the moment, not looking at her husband. She knew that he would have his closed, cold look and she preferred not to see it.

"How do you know someone feels anything if they can't show it?" Pauline warmed to her daughter-in-law.

"I expect your husband was a very compassionate man?" Anna asked.

"Was he, Ned?"

"Was he?" Ned asked himself. "He was marvelous with any wounded animal. That I do remember."

"Poor Toby," Pauline said.

"We had a dog who died of cancer," Ned explained. "Father nursed him, stayed up night after night with him." A thing, he also remembered, but did not say, was that it had irritated his mother. She felt the dog should have been put to sleep for mercy's sake and also because she didn't like Angus to sleep downstairs.

"Long, long ago," Pauline sighed. "Isn't memory a strange thing? A little thing makes an indelible impression. And then there are whole areas in the past that just disappear."

Anna was thinking what strange people these were . . . how close they came to coming out with things and then withdrew, as Ned now did. "All this is boring for Anna," he said.

"Not at all. I am fascinated. Do go on about your father."

"Ned never talks about his father," Pauline said. "Does anyone want a second helping? No? Well then, you may clear the table and bring in dessert, Maria."

Perhaps to change the subject, perhaps out of sheer curiosity, perhaps to stir things up, Pauline, using her new confidential tone with Anna, leaned toward her and whispered, "I'm always hoping for some good news."

"What's that, Mother?" Ned's voice was sharp. "To what good news are you referring?"

"I give you three guesses," she said, smiling across at her son.

"I'll give you good news. Anna had a triumph in Pittsburgh last week."

"You know that isn't what I meant! Though I am very glad to hear it, of course."

But this playing around, cat and mouse, did not appeal to Anna. "Your mother hopes to hear I am pregnant, Ned."

"You see, she knows." Pauline dove into her lemon meringue pie with enthusiasm. "Well?"

"Beulah is a genius," Ned said, after a mouthful.

Anna waited for help, but when none was forthcoming and Ned did not glance her way, she decided to speak out for once, for once come out as her real self. "I'm afraid you will be disappointed, Mrs. Fraser. Perhaps you should know that we do not intend to have children. I am thirty-six."

"That's not too late these days."

"Let it be, Mama," Ned was clearly upset, upset and angry.

"Well, it doesn't seem strange to hope—I don't have a grandson."

"Oh, you are interested for purely selfish reasons."

"Selfish? You seem to me rather selfish. You are well off and brilliant, I am told. Anna is talented. It seems to me that you have an obligation *not* to decide against life."

"You sound like the Moral Majority, Mama." Ned was ice cold, Pauline was flushed. Anna, between them felt excruciatingly uncomfortable.

"Not at all. I am all for abortions for the poor, for some poor girl who gets pregnant by mistake and has no means to support a child. The rich, on the other hand, have a certain responsibility, it seems to me. But I know I am old-fashioned," she added in a gentler tone. "A dodo who still believes in family life."

Anna was so afraid that Ned would attack his mother, who had not created anything like what is normally thought of as "family life" for Paul and him, that she plunged in recklessly, cutting him off as he said "Mama!" in a furious tone.

"It's my fault, Mrs. Fraser. I do not believe that I can serve my gift as it must be served and bring up a child." It sounded so pompous that Anna cringed as she heard herself saying it. How could one say such a thing? How could it ring true? And to be compelled to make such a statement offended her deeply. Once again she was being forced out of what such people considered normal into some wild fantasy that seemed to them outlandish if not actually criminal.

"Well, in that case . . . "

"Mama," Ned realized that Anna was in a difficult position. "Mama," he said again to get her attention. "When I was a bachelor I was constantly under attack . . . you needled me, didn't you? You said almost the same things then, that with all my advantages, etc. I had an obligation to marry. Isn't it time that we all accepted that there is not only one way to the good life and that family life is not the be-all and end-all of human endeavor?" And astonishing himself, he reached across the table to clasp Anna's ice-cold hand for a moment.

"Most people would agree with your mother," she said.

"It doesn't seem strange," Mrs. Fraser said, "to wish to see the world populated with intelligent people! There are enough underprivileged arriving every day to add to our taxes and live lives of penury." She said it with such complacency that it was followed by silence.

"Well, let's have our coffee on the porch," she signalled Maria and they got up, but even settled in the sunny informal room, the mood was now not to be broken.

"You are evading the issue, Mama, with all that talk of populating the world with an elite, a frightfully snobbish point of view. I won't argue. That is not the issue."

"But if the issue is not that, what is it?" Pauline Fraser asked with extreme politeness. It seemed to her quite unforgivable to have been attacked in this way.

"The issue," Anna said coldly, "is art, Mrs. Fraser. Maybe it's easier for men . . . most male singers are married and their wives bring up families, but for a woman it's much harder. Can't you see? I am on the road much of the time, and when I am not, I work hard rehearsing."

"But surely you are depriving yourself . . . and Ned." Mrs. Fraser would not have admitted it, but she was enjoying what she thought of as a battle of wits. Two against one at that, but she was holding her own.

"Maybe I am. But Ned knew who I was when he married me."

"I fell in love with a singer, Mama, not with a cow!" At this he laughed and exchanged a glance with Anna, but she could not respond to his laughter. She felt too vulnerable, too exposed.

"It's all beyond me, I'm afraid . . . " Pauline Fraser felt tired. After all, how could she win? "I always thought artists were first of all great human beings," she murmured.

"And it is necessary for a woman to bear children to be a great human being?" Ned was relentless.

"It seems unnatural not to . . . "

"The fact is," Anna's voice rose, "that one pays a high price for even a small talent—and that is what no one understands. Oh, if I could only make it clear . . . " Anna was close to tears now. After all, perhaps she *was* depriving Ned. "We do what we can Mrs. Fraser. I don't know whether I shall ever really make it to the top. . . . But that's the risk, and if I say so myself, it is not ignoble to be willing to risk so much!" she said passionately, too passionately.

"You are a very powerful woman, Anna! You are so sure of yourself, of a destiny I suppose. It is hard for an ordinary old woman to understand you." The false tone jarred.

"Sure of myself?" Anna was shaking now, with anger or pain it was hard to tell. "Don't you know I am a mass of self-doubt? That I have to face it and get over it every day?"

"Please don't shout. I'm not deaf." Maria was standing in the doorway with the coffee tray and hesitated to come in. "Come in, Maria. Cream? Sugar?" Pauline asked Anna.

"Black, please." The coffee was poured and passed by Maria and while she was in the room, the amenities were preserved. When she had left, Anna said coldly, "I'm sorry to be such a disappointment." Why had she even tried to explain? Why had she let herself get angry?

Ned had refused coffee and taken refuge in the kitchen where he was congratulating Beulah on her dinner. Sitting at the kitchen table with Pedro and about to eat, she was not responsive. "I do the best I can, Master Ned, but my legs ache after standing at the stove so long. I can't go on forever."

"No, I expect not. How long have you been with us?"

"Forty years. Believe it or not." Then she smiled a slow smile. "I can remember you when you were in diapers."

"Imagine that," said Pedro, giving Ned a wink. "Come on, Maria, your chops are getting cold!"

"I must go back to the gloom and doom," Ned said.

"She gets worse . . . but you should come more often, Master Ned. Perks her up. I could hear you arguing at the table. That's all right. She needs someone to tell her off once in a while." Beulah frowned, "It's loneliness . . . "

"Yes. Well, we're all lonely when it comes to that!"

"It's a long haul, that's all." And Beulah, anxious to eat in peace, dismissed him with that.

"Where have you been, Ned?" Mrs. Fraser asked plaintively. "Your coffee's getting cold."

"Just talking to Beulah for a minute."

"I hope she's over her cross mood. She's quite impossible these days."

"Her legs ache, Mama."

"They always have," said Pauline Fraser.

Ned chuckled. "You two . . . it's like a crotchety marriage. I wonder why it's lasted forty years."

"She's loyal, and so am I," Pauline said, with a lift of her chin. "Besides, I couldn't do without her."

"Well, if you've finished your coffee, Anna, we'd better get going. I'll see if I can find Fonzi . . . " and he walked down to the garden, whistling. Fonzi was fast asleep under a rose bush, but leapt up, delighted to be noticed at last.

Anna and Pauline Fraser stood in the doorway watching them play together, Fonzi chasing a stick, Ned throwing it again and again.

"He's just like his father. All that feeling about a dog!"

But Anna was not going to give at this point.

"Goodbye, Anna. I hope you have success in Dallas."

At last, Anna felt as she ran down to join Ned and Fonzi, we are out of the cage.

They walked down the path, pausing at the gate to wave. Mrs. Fraser was still standing in the doorway and waved back without smiling. They have each other, she thought, and I have no one. But I'll never understand why Ned married her. She's so intense! So self-absorbed!

"Why do I do it, Ned?" Anna asked when they had got back and were packing up to go back to the city. They were standing in the kitchen, Anna unrolling plastic to wrap the remains of the roast in, Ned emptying the frigidaire of milk and orange juice.

"What do you do? Mother is simply an impossible woman!"

"No . . . why do I shout and scream, why do I have to be so on the defensive?"

"Well, thank God you didn't scream!" Ned teased.

"I'm so uncomfortable on a social occasion. . . . It's ridiculous, isn't it?"

For some reason, perhaps that he resented his mother so much, Anna was not on the defensive now with Ned. She felt that for once he was on her side. How strange, how out of the ordinary that was!

"Well, in this case we were both attacked. I was just as angry as you were."

"Were you? Were you really?"

"It's none of her damned business whether we have children or not!"

"No . . ." Anna set the roast in the basket, took a couple of closed containers from Ned and set them in it. Then she burst into tears. Standing there at the counter, she began to weep uncontrollably.

"What's all this about?" Ned said, handing her a Kleenex. But she was unable to speak. Her tears had now turned to painful sobs. "I feel like a m-m-monster," she sobbed. "It's true what your mother said . . . I'm selfish and . . ."

"Should be shot at dawn," Ned used her own phrase to make her see how silly she was being. "Anna, you simply must not let mother do this to you!"

Anna blew her nose. "It's not your mother . . . I mean, maybe she is right . . . oh, Ned!" She turned to him and saw him through a blur of tears, and for a second leaned against him, her head on his shoulder. But Ned did not, could not hold her in his arms. Anna's tears froze him. "It's so lonely," she said, "I feel like an orphan."

"You're not an orphan, so why make up this fantasy that you are one? I simply cannot understand you, Anna." He took the basket and went out to the garage with it. What a mess of a day it had turned into! It was always a mistake to go to his mother's and today had turned into a disaster. What did Anna mean about an "orphan"? Or was she in her crazy way feeling that a woman with no child was an orphan? A ludicrous concept at best. Women were such biological constructs . . . everything appeared to come from and go back to the womb. But he had imagined that Anna was powerful enough not to allow herself this sort of indulgence. She did not want a child. Why not have the guts to stand by that fact without an orgy of self-pity?

When he went back into the house Anna was upstairs closing the suitcases, as she called down to tell him. So he went up, and without a word took the cases out. Anna, he noted with relief, had stopped crying.

In the last few minutes she had reached a cold clarity at the center of confusion: I simply have to work now and forget everything else. Even Ned.

And in the car with Fonzi asleep between them she touched Ned's arm gently and said, "It was nice when you played for me last night, and I sang . . . darling, thank you."

"It was very enjoyable," Ned answered. "We should do it more often. I'm going to have the piano tuned while you're away."

"Greater love hath no man," she teased, and as spontaneously as she had wept a half an hour ago, she laughed her loud delightful laugh.

How could one believe she was not acting all the time if she could seem to be in despair one moment and the next burst into such carefree laughter?

"I can't see that I made a joke," Ned said stiffly. "But I'm always happy to amuse you."

"*You* are the joke," Anna said, still smiling. "You are such an absurd man." She looked at him out of the corner of her eye. "But you are quite right. The piano does need tuning."

Chapter XIII

Anna's moment of rage and acute grief on the weekend had released pent up powers. Even Protopova was for once pleased with her work on the *Kindertoten lieder.* The Fauré songs she had sung many times and they hardly needed work. And at Anna's suggestion they spent two mornings trying out some works she might consider for future concerts: three Beethoven songs, a setting by Duparc of Baudelaire, and finally Glück's *Orpheus.*

There were fittings for a new dress. The question of dress for the morning musicales did present a problem. Anna felt more at ease in a long dress, but this time she had found a cocktail dress, panné velvet of a rather subtle shade of lavenderish blue that she could feel at ease wearing at eleven in the morning . . . if only Dallas was not in the middle of a heat wave!

It was one of those weeks when Ned had several business or professional dinners, as well as a game of tennis with Johnny, so Anna invited Teresa over one evening for a homey meal at the apartment, fettucini and a salad. Getting it ready was rather fun. Fonzi, who had a neurotic fear of the slippery kitchen floor, lay at the doorsill with his nose just over the edge, hoping for a taste of something before she was through. And Anna talked to him while she worked.

"Aren't you glad we don't have to go to a boring dinner and talk about money, Fonzi? Poor Ned! But why do I say that, Fonzi? You and I know that he loves it. It's his life, after all. It's what he knows everything about and people come from all over the world just to find out what Ned thinks is going to happen. Will we have a recession? What is to be done about bonds? Imagine knowing the answers to all that, Fonzi!"

Fonzi looked rather anxious, not about the market, but as to whether the piece of cheese he knew was still on the counter would vanish before he had a taste.

"I haven't forgotten you!" And Anna cut the cheese into five little pieces, "even though we have to admit you are a stout little dog and hardly in need of food!"

Anna and her mother were apt to meet at lunchtime so it seemed quite an occasion to be having supper together here in the apartment. And Anna, who rarely thought much about such things, enjoyed setting the table with beautiful Chinese plates, the best Steuben glasses, and as centerpiece a few tiny yellow roses.

"There, Fonzi, we are ready."

Anna was standing at the window looking out at the Common and its twinkling lights far below, wondering if the apartment would ever really feel like home. After two years it still felt unlived in, unloved in, she found herself saying. And she knew the warmth had to come from inside . . . would it ever? There was love—she didn't doubt that—but it was in a strange way not operative.

"Oh, Mama," she opened the door to Teresa's buzz and enfolded the slight figure in a bear hug. "I'm so glad to see you!"

Teresa extricated herself and laughed. "You don't have to strangle me to tell me that, do you?"

Anna lit the fire, for Teresa was shivering, and explained that there was an icy wind outside. "There, sit in the little chair and warm your hands while I make the drinks. The usual for you, Mama?"

"Oh, any old wine you might have open—you know me!"

While Anna was in the kitchen Teresa patted Fonzi and looked around. For some reason this room had never felt like Anna and she had often wondered what was missing. Of course it was all in frightfully good taste, but where did Anna really live? In the music room, maybe. They had sacrificed a guest room so that Anna could have her baby grand and a place to work.

"Well, you are looking like yourself, I'm glad to see," she said when Anna came back.

"And that means like a tramp?" For Anna had on an old pair of slacks and a blue turtleneck sweater.

"No, darling one, I meant looking on top of things for a change, less like a beaten dog, more like . . . "

"Not like a beaten dog, Mama, surely not," Anna broke in. "I've never been a beaten dog!"

"You looked dimmed . . . I don't know . . . it made me quite anxious. Did that knockdown fight you mentioned really help? It puzzles me that you seem to think anger is a good thing."

"Does it?" Anna frowned. "I guess I think anything open and played out is healthier than anything closed off and buried."

"I wonder . . . "

"Ned said awful things to me, Mama. He said I was selfish."

Teresa smiled. "Sometimes you are selfish . . . "

"Mama!"

"Well, aren't you? You put your music first, after all. I can see that a husband might feel that was selfish."

"Damn it, Mama, he knew that when he married me!" Anna got up. "It is not selfish to serve an art! You sound like Mrs. Fraser!"

"God forbid!"

"Never mind," Anna pushed her hair back with an impatient gesture and sat down again, "What I wanted to say when I got sidetracked was that—this will shock you, but I can't help it—I was glad he said all the things he did. There was a real excitement in our shouting at each other. It cleared the air, and the proof is that we are not as irritated as we were. When he got so angry I really loved him."

"Well, all I can say is that you are a strange woman."

Teresa had always been honest with her daughter. The strength of their relationship rested partly on that. Anna knew exactly where she was with her mother; she knew that she was accepted totally, but also that her mother was quite clear about faults and shortcomings.

"What I can't stand is the way Ned hides from me and from himself. I feel so baffled, Mama, when he is cold and I don't know what I have done!"

"What you have done is to be critical and angry. Isn't that so, my little dragon?"

Anna looked up, met her mother's perceptive eyes, and smiled a rueful smile. "Maybe so. Sometimes I think I should never have married. I'm such an impossible person."

"Possible, but improbable," Teresa chuckled and Anna laughed.

"What makes the anger, Mama? Why am I so angry?" Anna regretted the question as soon as she had uttered it. Why go naked? "Why am I so vulnerable?" she whispered.

Teresa was silent for a moment. "I often asked myself that question when you were small . . . it seemed then as though whatever you wanted you wanted almost too intensely. You reacted to any frustration so fast, like lightning."

"I know. That rabbit at Filene's. I made an awful scene when you wouldn't get it for me."

"It was five-feet high, Anna!"

Anna couldn't help laughing and Teresa laughed too, till tears streamed down their cheeks while she spoke in gasps "You lay on the floor, screaming . . . " then she pulled herself together. "Why are we laughing? It was appalling, an unforgivable scene. I was dreadfully embarrassed."

"Poor Mama, I was a handful . . . "

"A handful? You were an armful! More . . . a trained elephant could not have controlled your passion at times." She drank the end of her wine and set the glass down thoughtfully. "Your father diagnosed it as a kind of illness, a fit, as it were."

"Did he? Oh dear . . . " This Anna had not heard before. "Cold, angry people can never understand hot, angry people. Father hadn't the foggiest idea what I was all about. What I needed was love not punishment."

"Yes, I think I knew that—but darling, it is quite hard to love someone who screams at you! And your father was such a reserved man himself."

"The screamer is always wrong," Anna felt a burning shame inside. "I suppose that is why I am so vulnerable . . . I know I am awful but I can't help it. It's part of me, don't you see? Without it I couldn't sing as I do."

"When you are angry your eyes are black, black, not blue."

"Are they?"

"And I have sometimes imagined that blackness was the daimon in you taking over, the daimon you can't control."

"And never expect."

"Should the daimon be tamed? Can the daimon be tamed?" Teresa said gently. "It's not easy to be you, is it, Anna?" She reached over and took Anna's hand and held it in her two.

"Compassion, Mama," Anna had tears in her eyes. "You feel it because you are my mother. Ned can't."

"When you are attacked it is not easy to feel compassion for your attacker, Anna. Do you feel it for him?"

"Sometimes I do. I do when I see his mother and realize

how awful his childhood was. I do when he says he can't give . . . it seems so terrible not to be able to give."

"He does, Anna. In his own way."

"Mama," Anna sat up straight, severe suddenly. "He can't say a loving word. He has never given me a lover's present. He can't even wish me luck before a concert!"

"Well, it's hard for you. I can see that. You are such a verbal person and it's so easy for you to express your feelings, but that is the way he is, Anna. He is not going to change."

"I know. I know that. That is why I am in pain so much of the time, beating my head against a wall . . . "

"Let me say just one thing, Anna, and then we must have something to eat. I'm starving."

"Go ahead . . . improbable I may be, but I have made you a delicious supper."

"I have sometimes thought that you need someone to battle, that your nature demands someone to be pitted *against.* And that is why, perhaps, you fell in love with Ned. Would you want to be married to an adorer who gave you all you wanted without question?"

"He says all my friends are sycophants! He thinks that is what I do want—and because he thinks that, he buttons himself up against ever praising me. It's mean."

"I wonder . . . " Teresa was thinking this over. "I think you forget, Anna, what a powerful personality you are. Perhaps he is afraid he will be simply taken over altogether if he yields, even a little."

At this Anna laughed, it seemed so preposterous. Most of the time she felt if not weak exactly, so set outside what anyone could love or want. Powerful? But she had come to the end of what she could say to her mother and went out into the kitchen and got the meal together, and for the rest of the evening it was a little bask of pleasure, pleasure in the fettucini, in the wine, and in sharing it for once.

Over coffee by the fire, Anna said, "It's awful how I never see you, Mama! I seem to be always running these days . . . there's never time for anything except work. I'm on a roller coaster—after Dallas the same program in San Francisco ten days later!"

"It's all beginning to happen, isn't it? All you have worked for, all you have dreamed."

"What I dream of now is singing *Orpheus,* in London, maybe Glyndebourne."

"In the past two years you have grown—you seem to be in touch with greater powers, deeper. I think Ned is good for you."

"A healthy struggle—if we don't both die of it!" Anna laughed.

They talked a few moments then about Dan Weaver, Anna's accompanist, a young man just emerging from years at the conservatory.

"I think he rather enjoys these concerts, at least as an interim. He needs the money. And one of these days he'll be off and away on his own career. Meanwhile I am lucky to have him."

"And Ned is not jealous?"

"Of course not. Dan has a friend, a tenor. He's quite safe, Mama."

"Good."

"And he's very courteous and helpful. Besides we laugh at the same things, play scrabble—he's a charming companion."

It was time for Teresa to go. Anna called a cab and went downstairs with her to see her safely off. "Thanks, Mama," Anna said, kissing her mother goodbye.

Fonzi looked very disappointed when she got back. He wagged his tail furiously and barked. Anna picked him up and kissed his nose, "You have to wait, little dog, I wish I could take you for a walk but I can't. It's too dangerous. So we just have to be patient." She set him down and went into the kitchen to tidy things up. It was nearly ten and Ned should be home soon.

Anna, as usual when she had had a talk with her mother,

was feeling happy, at ease with herself, and when Ned came home she ran to the door and kissed him.

"Cold outside," he said, slipping his coat off. "Let's put another log on the fire. I could do with a brandy."

"Let's have one. Let's talk. I want to hear all about your dazzling dinner party!"

"Dazzling, it was not. No all male dinner party is ever dazzling," and Ned lifted his glass to Anna. Then he threw a log on the fire making a shower of sparks as it landed. Anna waited for him to get settled and put his feet up. She sensed that he too was feeling cheerful.

"It was rather an interesting evening, I must say. With the world economy in such a state, there's room for a lot of theorizing, a lot of speculation . . . "

"Do people ever come into it—the speculation—or is it all about gold?"

"It's all about people, Anna. The Third World is made up of millions of people existing way below the poverty level. And this has to be changed or we will all eventually go under. But try to tell that to the South Africans!"

"You really are powerful, aren't you?"

"Oh, we're small potatoes, and we have no overseas capital."

"Then why do these German banks and English banks come into the picture?"

"Because we have some of the same problems. The French banks are about to be nationalized—that has sent a shiver through the financial world."

For once Ned was willing to talk and Anna listened, happy to be included, happy that he would even try to explain his preoccupations. This was the Ned she rarely saw and hardly knew. He spoke quietly but she sensed the intensity of his commitment, as though thinking for Ned became a kind of electricity, an electric current, joining him up to a whole world. This was where he could feel fully himself as she did when she sang. He talked for quite a while, then he poured himself another brandy. "That's

enough about that," he said. "How was Teresa? Did you
have a good talk?"

"Yes, we did, Mama is the most truthful person I know."

"She's certainly a contrast to my mother," he said
grimly. "You know I think a lot about your childhood."

Then Anna suddenly laughed, "Mama reminded me
that I had thrown myself on the floor and screamed in
Filene's when I was about eight because she wouldn't give
me a five-foot stuffed rabbit!"

But Ned didn't even smile, and Anna was stopped short.

"What puzzles me," he said, "is why you think that's so
funny. It seems to me absolutely appalling—what did
your mother do?"

"Dragged me away."

"But what I can't understand is what made you think
you could have such a preposterous present? What made
you feel you had the right to ask for it, and to be furious
when you were denied it?"

"I wanted it so much . . . can't you see?"

Then Ned did smile. "You have the lowest threshhold
of frustration I have ever encountered! It seems to be a
little mad. I mean, after all, most people don't expect to
get what they want. Most people learn when they are
very young that life is not like that."

"I suppose they do," Anna said meekly.

"Life is apt to punish those who demand too much of
it." This time Ned was not angry and not cold, he was
interested. For him, Anna saw, it had become a philosoph-
ical question. "Weren't you punished?"

"I felt terrible afterwards thinking of how I had upset
Mama and how ashamed she was of me. I can't remember
whether I was punished or not."

"Wild hopes were always dashed for me as a child
. . . I learned to be very wary."

"Because if you let anyone know, the joy would be
taken away?"

"I guess so."

"Ah," Anna said, smiling at him, "that explains why you are so secretive."

Once more they were on the brink of a real talk but Ned withdrew with the excuse that it was high time he took Fonzi for a walk. "Want to come?"

"I don't dare, Ned . . . that icy wind! I can't risk catching cold with Dallas ahead."

"Very well, see you later," and Ned went off into the night with the dog.

When he got back Anna was still sitting by the dying fire.

"I thought you'd be in bed," he said, hanging up his coat. "It's after eleven."

"Is it?" Anna said. "I've been thinking . . . "

Ned winced. "We're not going to have a scene," he said, "I'm going to bed."

This, Anna recognized, was the climate she had created, a climate of fear if not actual antagonism. How would it ever be changed? And she heard her mother saying "Neither of you is going to change." What then? A lifetime of living on the surface, never talking about anything real? "Can't we keep the surfaces pleasant?" Ned had said plaintively long ago. But Anna knew that she could never accept that. What then? A lifetime of angry arguments that ended, at best, in a passionate "making up" in bed and at worst in withdrawal on both sides? Marriages are not made in heaven, Anna said to herself firmly, they are made in hell. When she finally slipped into bed in the dark, Ned was asleep. Fitting herself under his arm, feeling her breath drawn in and out in rhythm with his, and feeling Fonzi's warm body with her foot, Anna knew that, in spite of everything, because of everything, the union was ineluctable.

Chapter XIV

When a scene had been avoided, tension built up in Anna about whatever it was that had not been allowed to erupt. In the first year, Ned had seemed totally unaware of this, and taken by surprise when anger finally broke out. Now he had learned to be wary. He managed to leave for the office the next morning without more than a few casual words said.

Anna had been reluctant to accept a dinner invitation so close to her departure for Dallas, but had finally agreed to go out to Milton that night to the Faulkners. "It's not that I don't like them, Ned, it's only that I'm so close to that concert and don't want anything to happen."

"What could happen?"

"Anything could happen . . . a truck could run into us on the way home. Or I could lose my voice."

"You seem to build up anxiety as a necessary part of any performance. And the worse it gets the better you perform!"

"Let's drop it. I've said I'd go . . . " but as he picked up the *Times* for a glance at the business section, she added, "You've never realized, Ned, what these social occasions take out of me. I feel out of place and then it's such an immense effort . . . the energy expended in five or six hours of small talk!"

"I had an impression that the conversation at the Faulkners was exceptionally good. He has quite a flair for drawing people out . . . "

"Drawing you out, you mean!"

Ned smiled. "I guess I have to grant you that he isn't especially good at talking with women. . . . Well, I must be off. Take it easy."

"I have a lesson, you know." He was crazy to think she could take it easy these days.

But by then Ned was at the door. "See you at fiveish . . . " and he was gone.

He had gone out in a light overcoat and it was freezing out there, Anna thought. She sometimes imagined that Ned liked to be uncomfortable. It was part of the Bostonian ethos, not to coddle oneself even if a bad cold was the result!

"But you shall wear your coat, Fonzi, when I take you out. We can't have you catching a cold, can we?" and as Fonzi got out of his basket and wagged his tail hopefully, she patted his head. "And you believe in all the coddling you can get, don't you?

When Ned came home, Anna had tea ready and the fire lit. "Lovely—we don't have to dress for an hour. Lesson go well?" he asked.

"Soso."

"That tea was a splendid idea, Anna!"

"Ah," she stretched. Then lay on her back on the floor, her arms behind her head. "I've been thinking about you," she said.

"Possibly you might refrain from telling me what those thoughts were."

"But I want to tell you," Anna sat up. "It might even be interesting," she pleaded, reaching out a hand and touching his foot.

"Maybe I'm that five-foot rabbit you want and can't have."

"I can have it. I have to have it!" She was laughing now,

too. But then she sat back on her heels, rocking back and forth. "You never answer when I ask you what made you angry as a child and why you couldn't let the anger out."

"And now you think you know, Dr. Lindstrom?"

"Yes. I think I do know. I think you were terribly angry with your father for dying . . . and that was an anger you couldn't face. It had to be buried . . . "

Ned sipped his tea in silence. His face was a blank.

"Don't you see, that was the poison in your family . . . your mother was so angry at his death that she punished you and herself for years. It wasn't grief, Ned. You've never let the grief in. None of you ever did. Paul tried to kill himself he was so angry . . . you told me you didn't even cry!"

"Mother cried. She cried for years on every holiday! Mourning made me sick," Ned said coldly. "I can't see the point of this."

"But true mourning isn't self-pity and isn't anger," Anna said, amazed that all this had come into her head while she slept in those hours of the night when she had curled herself around Ned and knew that the union was real and deep. As though simple feeling had opened a door, had brought her closer to him than she had ever been.

"What is true mourning then? Can you tell me that?" The tone was irritable, but Anna paid no attention.

"Mourning?" She shook her head. "Perhaps I don't really know because I am only beginning—since we married—to be able to mourn my father."

"Since we married? What has that to do with your father?"

"Because, in some ways, I think you are rather like him."

"You are nothing like my mother, thank God!"

"Some day you will have to mourn her, too."

"Maybe, but I'm afraid my chief emotion will be relief."

"Ned!"

"Well, you talk about honesty all the time. I'm being honest."

"Mourning is letting the grief in . . . letting it *happen.* You loved your father and he abandoned you by dying. You used anger to shut the grief out, don't you see that's what you did?"

"Why are you so hell bent on digging all this up now?" Ned said. "We have to dress for dinner."

"We have an hour . . . I've got to get it straight, Ned. It's terribly important!"

"To you, maybe. But what makes you think I'll start mourning my father at this late date? He's been dead for years!"

"And you've buried your anger against him for years. So you talk about him as though he were a myth—and you almost never talk about him."

"It's too painful." Ned frowned and shook his head. "And you can't make me do it now." Anna reached over and held onto his foot. "Please let my foot alone."

"I want to hold some part of you, Ned. I want to touch you."

"You want to break me apart and take me over. You want to make me into you." He was in acute pain, breathing hard, Anna could see it. Once more anger was taking over from grief.

"What do you remember most clearly about your father?" she asked gently.

"That he said once that I didn't measure up—didn't measure up, Anna. That's what I remember now," and his voice sounded strangled.

"What had you done?"

"I hit Paul. He made me take the blame for letting the dog run away and I hit him hard."

"That must have been some satisfaction."

"Paul always baited me. He *wanted* me to break out. He was older, you see, and he always managed to win."

"But it's quite preposterous, Ned . . . can't you see? Your

father didn't know what had really happened."

"No, he didn't. But he would have said the same thing if he had, 'You don't measure up.' I've spent years trying to forget that, bury it. Why did you make me say it?"

"I didn't. You chose to remember that, you chose anger and pain rather than love. But you don't have to. You have measured up. If your father were here with us now he would be bursting with pride. You are far more successful than he ever was."

"Success didn't interest him. Character did. You had to be a good person."

"And what is a good person?"

Ned closed his eyes. "A good person," he said as though he had learned the words by heart, "is self-controlled, does not indulge in self-pity, is cheerful, and harder on himself than on others."

"Everything negative, except cheerful," Anna murmured. "And a good person always has to be right."

"You are right if you behave well."

"Yes," Anna thought this over for a moment. "But maybe a good person has to be vulnerable enough to be wrong sometimes."

"Would your father have agreed with that?" Ned shot back.

"Of course not." Anna was close to tears herself. "My father didn't understand anything about people, about himself or anyone else."

"Yet the marriage worked, you tell me."

"It worked because my mother gave in, never fought for what she believed, just did whatever would make him happy."

"She seems very serene."

"She made her peace, but is that what life is all about? Peace at any price?"

Ned smiled a grim smile. "Not to you. You want war at any price."

"I want understanding. I want to grow. I want to let the

pain in and use it. I won't build walls. I won't hide behind walls!" Anna said passionately.

"But do you mourn your father now? And has it really something to do with me, with us?" In spite of himself, she could see that Ned was interested, more stirred up than he wanted to be, himself now needing to talk. Was it because he sensed a change in her? She was not attacking him this time, not at least in the same way as before, as though she needed to break him down to be herself. He had ceased to be the enemy. She lifted her eyes and met his.

"My father was hard on me," she said, "but I'm beginning to see that I was hard on him, especially after I was grown up. I used to fight him about nearly everything and I hurt him, Ned."

"Yes, I imagine you may have . . . you are powerful when you are angry, more powerful than you know."

"I have hurt you, too."

"Yes, you have."

Tears poured down Anna's cheeks and she brushed them off, too concentrated to care. "I think what I am beginning to see is that someone as strong and controlled as my father was, is in some way helpless and so terribly afraid of being found out . . ."

"How helpless? A neurologist has to be pretty tough . . . and awfully sure of himself."

"He seemed sure of himself," Anna murmured. "But with me as a child he fumbled and he must have known that he did. If you arouse hatred in your child, something must boomerang back onto you, inside you. Oh Ned, I couldn't forgive him—even when he was dying. Why am I telling you all this?"

"Because . . ." Ned found it difficult to put what he was sensing into words, "mourning is forgiving . . . is that it? I mean, all this began about mourning, how anger shuts mourning out."

"Oh darling," Anna reached across and clasped Ned's

hand, "Thank God I don't have to mourn you!"

"So you don't have to forgive me?" he smiled.

"Please talk about your father now," she said. She sensed that the time had come for Ned, for them both, when he could.

Ned leaned back then in his chair, looking up at the ceiling. "He was so alive, Anna! Every bit of him was so alive . . . just the way he built a fire for a picnic, just the way he laughed. Everything seemed possible when he was there. As a boy I felt his challenge like a spur. He taught me to sail when I was only seven and terrified of scrambling around in a rough sea. But when I was seasick he held my head while I threw up . . . I've always remembered that, for some reason . . . I guess because he wasn't affectionate in the usual way. He was very shy. But when he was pleased with me, he used to ruffle my hair."

"He was a real father," Anna said.

"I think he was lonely," Ned sat up. "He tried so hard to make us a happy family, reading Dickens aloud around the fire, things like that, but . . ." Ned rubbed his forehead as he did when he was troubled, "but I guess the best times we had were outdoors when he could do things with us alone." There was a silence. Then something broke. Ned didn't sound like his usual self. He was almost shouting, and as he spoke he pounded the arm of his chair with his fist. "He shouldn't have died so young—he was only forty. How could he go like that? How could he do it to us?"

"It was an accident, surely?"

"That is what we were told."

"You don't believe it?"

Ned stared at her, a blank stare of amazement. This is what he had shut out all those years, refused to admit. And now he was saying it quite coldly. "I feel certain that it was suicide."

"Why? Why believe the worst? Cars do go out of control."

"Not my father's car." Ned pulled himself up and walked up and down. Was he aware that he was shouting? "He left us in total darkness, Anna! How could he do that? He knew what Mama was . . . he knew he was leaving us alone, horribly alone! The door was closed on us two little boys, forever! Oh, Anna, the darkness!"

Anna got up and went to him and held him in her arms, while Fonzi, who had never heard Ned shout, ran round and round barking. But for once Ned paid no attention to the dog. "I'll never get over it, Anna," he was weeping. "I'll never be well."

"Maybe that's what your father felt—maybe that's why . . ." Anna wiped his tears with the palm of her hand very gently. "Does it have to go on from generation to generation, the closing off, the fear of feeling?"

"We're way out somewhere on a limb," Ned extricated himself and blew his nose. "Good heavens, Anna, we have to dress for dinner . . . we'll be late!"

"Just a second! We're not out on a limb, Ned. Or if we are, we're out there together."

"O.K., but I'd rather be safe." Ned had resumed his shell, but it didn't matter. And Anna, getting into a red dress, felt strangely at peace. She realized that they had become friends in the last hour. And even if this moment of truth didn't last, could not be sustained, it was there like a touchstone. Ned had let her in at last.

Chapter XV

The day after Anna left for Dallas, Ned made a sudden decision, as he walked across the Common to his office. Why analyze, he told himself when the voice of conscience suggested that he had no business cancelling a meeting. Does a squirrel analyze why he feels compelled to gather nuts for the winter? The squirrels on the Common that morning had been in a frenzy of activity; one had made him laugh aloud as it used a cigarette wrapper to cover a cache, and stamped on it, with furious energy. Had Ned ever followed an impulse with as little regard for appearances as this impulse he was about to follow? Yes, he smiled at himself, when I asked Anna to marry me.

"Miss Prior," he said briskly, "get me a flight to Dallas for tonight after work. Dinner on the plane if possible, to return Thursday afternoon. Get me a hotel, too, central—I don't want to be somewhere in the suburbs."

"Very well, Mr. Fraser."

"Oh yes . . ." Ned said, putting on his glasses and scanning the morning mail, opened and waiting on his desk. "That meeting tomorrow. It's a nuisance, but you'll have to tell the board it has to be delayed till Friday. Something has come up."

"Anything else?"

"No thanks."

When Miss Prior had left, Ned sat there for a moment wondering whether he was crazy. But he hadn't heard Anna sing for over a year—wasn't it natural to be pulled toward seeing her—and hearing her—where nothing jarred and all was composed, whole, and full of magic? The Anna who entranced and consoled? His Anna—and at the same time, Anna Lindstrom, not his at all? Perhaps the impulse felt so strong because he needed to see her again at a distance . . . but that was enough analyzing for Ned and he plunged into the day's affairs and, the decision made, worked with an extra edge of excitement and pleasure.

Miss Prior heard Ned whistling and was quite astonished. He was a considerate employer, was almost never out of temper, had a wry sense of humor which she enjoyed, but otherwise was extremely reticent and reserved. After five years in his employ she knew next to nothing about him. He didn't even have a photograph of his wife in the office and had never mentioned her name. But he had seemed excited about Dallas. What could be happening in Dallas?

Meanwhile Ned had suddenly remembered that something must be done about Fonzi and called Teresa. "I am called away on business and Anna, of course, will be in Dallas. Could you possibly take Fonzi for twenty-four hours? Don't tell Anna—I don't want anything to make her nervous on this trip, and she might worry."

"I won't say a word." It did cross Teresa's mind that it was all a little odd. Was Ned meeting another woman somewhere? But Teresa had to admit that for all the tensions in this marriage, neither Ned nor Anna had ever looked at anyone else, as far as she knew. They seemed pretty much absorbed in whatever was going on between them, even when it was chiefly rage.

On the plane Ned leaned back and closed his eyes. He felt he had been running all day. His mind was brilliantly lit up and he couldn't stop thinking, stop running, even now safely on the plane and on his way. It seemed as though memory was a ribbon flying backward at incredible speed, back through the flotsam and jetsam of the day (he had gone home to pack his suitcase at lunchtime and hand Fonzi over to Teresa), back through the week to the long talk with Anna which he had laid aside deliberately, not allowed himself to think about until this moment in limbo, back through thirty-years, to his father. There was no stopping the unrolling of the ribbon now. And the double Scotch he ordered only accelerated it.

It came to a full stop with the word "suicide." "My father committed suicide. My father committed suicide. My father committed suicide." It was such an explosive sound in his head that Ned looked around nervously as though the intensity of it must be heard by the other passengers, the bearded young man reading Vonnegut in the seat beside him. But of course only he, Ned, could hear those words or say them. He closed his eyes. Why was he so sure that that was the truth? At ten years old what had he seen or sensed that made him know it, and then bury it until the other night when it sprang out, sprang out to Anna? For years he had chosen to remember his father only as "so alive" as he always said, as what could only be called a father figure, splendid, all powerful, wise, and always making good things happen for Ned and Paul. What had he buried? Something positively known or seen?

His father had been absolutely self-assured, in command of himself—so it had seemed to a boy of ten. But now Ned was a man of forty-two, the same age his father had been when he died, he realized suddenly that the man was aware of things the boy sensed but could not quite understand . . . for one, his mother's irritation when his father sat up night after night with their sick dog. He felt that was rather mean of his mother, he remembered, but what came back now was the violence of his father's reaction. The fury and pain with which he said, "I'm just not adequate, Pauline. I'm not what you need," and walked out to the office without his breakfast.

Not adequate? Could a human being have this feeling about himself even when the facts proved it quite untrue? "Not adequate." . . . For the first time in his life Ned began to think about his father not as his father, but as a man in the midst of a life that his son could know very little about. Under the genial, fun-loving, life-enhancing man had there been despair? Once in a while the boys were told that their father was sick in bed and must not be disturbed. "He has a migraine headache," their mother explained. "Please don't make any noise when you come back from school."

But was it a migraine or was it an attack of excruciating self-doubt? Self-doubt why and about what? What made Ned suddenly remember that he had heard that his father started out after college at the bank where Pauline's father was president . . . he must have gotten out when the boys were quite small, and become business manager then of a small firm, really a one-man show, which made stained glass windows for churches and public buildings. The "one-man" of the show was an eccentric geniusy craftsman who was in love with the Gothic and designed and worked with three or four workmen he had trained. Apprentices came and went. As a business it was distinguished enough but rather small potatoes. Ned imagined now that it must have been a kind of escape hatch for his father, something valid from a professional view but far from the center of power the bank had represented. Had his father somehow not measured up at the bank? Or had a fight with his father-in-law? At forty did he feel he was a failure? Had he wanted to be a writer or an artist of some sort himself, but felt pressured by marrying a fortune into

a semblance at least of success in the business world? Oh,
Ned groaned inwardly, if I only knew.

What he did know was that under the surface his father
was locked up inside. The whole business of "measuring
up" had to do with not complaining, with never imposing
personal matters on anyone even, Ned surmised, on his
wife. Ned had learned quite early on that any talk of being
cross or depressed or in any way unable to cope, was
treated as a sin. You had to be amused, have fun, enjoy
. . . and his father had been so good at inventing ways to
have fun that it seemed quite natural to put down any soul
searching as self-indulgent. Now Ned began to see that
that, just that was self-protection and under the surface
may have lived a man in pain, an excruciatingly lonely
man, in the end a mortally sick man.

"Are we very rich, Papa?" he had asked his father once
when they were climbing Mount Monadnock on the October 12th holiday. "Johnny says we are."

His father had walked on without answering, he
remembered, and only later when they were eating a
sandwich at the top, had closed the subject with the
words, "I wouldn't worry, Ned. We have enough to live
on."

"I wasn't worried," Ned said, throwing pebbles one by
one.

It seemed a little strange that money was never talked
about. Only vulgar people expressed any interest in it,
Ned learned and when later on he complained that other
boys at school were given far larger allowances than either he or Paul his father had expressed surprise. "I don't
see what you need money for at school, except to show
off."

"I want ski boots, Father."

"Well, save up for a few months."

Ned had sensed that it would be wiser to leave it at that.

But suicide? None of all this explained it. Except . . . the
idea came to him with force like an explosion . . . if no

deep feelings find a way of expression, if anger is taboo, if admitting depression is a sin, if even love is expressed only by things done, never things said—then what happens to a human being? "Does it have to go on from generation to generation?" he heard Anna's voice in his head, "The closing off? The fear of feeling?"

How did she know when he did not know himself? Had his father's sense of impotence cut him off finally even from his wife? Ned winced. No child can imagine his parents in bed and even now at forty he screened off what he had just imagined. A man cut off from everything except nursing a sick dog . . . so when the dog died, the death had become an immense hazard, gone the only love that could be expressed, gone the only way out for tenderness and compassion. That at least explained his mother's irritations. Oh no, Ned told himself, that's crazy. Absolutely crazy. People don't commit suicide over a dog! No, he told himself, people kill themselves when they are so cut off from whatever their real life is or could be that there is nowhere else to go.

Ned was jolted out of his strange state of awareness by the physical jolt of the plane landing. It was quite a relief to get out of that cocoon where he had been so close to his father, when he had seen him for the first time since his death as a person in his own right, to be on his way back from so far, toward life lived at full intensity—Anna!

Chapter XVI

Anna woke next morning to a fine day in Dallas. She felt
well, for once not too nervous, but she had worked on this
concert as hard as she ever had on anything, and maybe,
she thought, I am at last learning to trust myself, my voice,
and go into a concert happy and assured. Was that possible? It was easier to sing at eleven in the morning, not
have to live through a whole nervous day, get it over with
while she had the morning freshness still about her . . . it
would not be too hot, she had heard on the radio, and that,
too, added to her sense of well-being. So she called Dan
in his room, and could not help laughing when he con-
fessed that he had slept badly and was a bit panicky. "Dan!
For once I'm not . . . it went so well last night. Are you
still bothered about the piano?"

"Maybe," he said. "I couldn't feel a quite perfect rap-
port with it, I must say."

"But you played beautifully!"

"Oh well, I expect it will be all right. I won't make an
ass of myself, Anna. I promise."

"I wonder whether it will be a good house . . . they said
they were selling tickets but couldn't be sure ahead of
time of a sellout. Apparently it's rather rare for the club
to open its doors to strangers, and I presume they did it
this time because we have become rather expensive."

"Well, your name should pull in a crowd . . . I wouldn't
worry."

"I don't have a name, Dan. How would anyone in Dallas
know I exist?"

"Come on, Anna, I refuse to flatter you. Did you see the
piece in the paper this morning? That should pull them
in!"

"It was quite surprisingly impressive," Anna said. Indeed she had read it with astonishment. "Someone did a
lot of sleuthing. I hardly recognized myself."

"You're either very modest or quite stupid. Take your
choice," Dan teased.

"Let's have fun, Dan! I'll meet you downstairs at ten.
They are sending a limousine to take us over."

When she put the phone down, Anna was tingling all
over with excitement. Now if she could just hold onto it,
walk the tightrope until she was on the stage! Not fall into
a panic.

She poured herself a second cup of coffee and sipped it
slowly, sitting up straight. One of her anxieties had always
been choking on something just before a concert—that, or
slipping in the shower and breaking a leg. Anxiety came
in all shapes and sizes, but today she was able to keep it
at bay. And that, she realized, was because she did not feel
as acutely alone as she often did just before a performance. Whatever had happened between her and Ned was
giving her a new sense of support, of his being there at her
side. So new that she was afraid to think about it for fear
it would vanish.

Meanwhile, an hour later, Ned was making his way into
the auditorium through a bevy of talkative women, as far
as he could see, the only man among them. He thought
of Ernesta Aldrich and wished devoutly that she were
there at his side to give him at least the appearance of
belonging. His seat was on the aisle in the tenth row.
Perhaps he could pretend to be a critic? And with that in
mind he took out a pen and studied the program atten-

tively. He imagined Anna and Dan waiting nervously in the wings—that last fifteen minutes, Anna had often told him, was the real hell.

Someone came out and opened the grand piano, turned on the keyboard light, and arranged the music. It was a rather charming stage, not too big, with a background of beige velvet curtains and, as he looked around, Ned was impressed by the elegance of the auditorium, and smiled at his own provincialism, the Bostonian idea of Dallas being something a little more showy and less distinguished. But then the women all around him were pretty distinguished-looking themselves, with the exception of a few college students, not members of the club, he surmised, in the usual boots, blue jeans and ragged bulky sweaters. What would it be like to step out and meet an audience like this, buzzing with excitement? How to bring it together and silence it like some wild animal to be tamed with a glance? Ned looked at his watch. It was past eleven. It occurred to him that this was a very different occasion to that day three years ago when he had expected nothing much and did not know that in five minutes his life was to be radically changed. Now his expectation was high but also he was nervous *for* Anna and with her . . . he was involved. And the involvement made him impatient and critical. Why didn't they get on with it? Every seat appeared to be taken. He felt Anna's tension inside himself.

Then at last a woman appeared with a sheaf of papers in her hand, evidently the president of the club. She had some announcements to make, apologized for keeping the audience even a moment from "the treat" ahead, and finally when Ned's exasperation had reached a dangerous point, launched into a prepared introduction of Anna Lindstrom which she read rather haltingly, but with emphasis. "We are indeed fortunate to welcome to Dallas this morning, the magnificent Anna Lindstrom."

Where was Anna? The lady hesitated, then made her

way to the wings, as the audience applauded, and only then Anna walked out onto the stage, followed by Dan. Ned breathed a sigh of relief. There she was indeed, her eyes shining, making several bows, her smile encompassing the whole hall in that magic way she had, then fading very suddenly as her eyes saw Ned. He had not meant to be seen, not meant to have the effect his presence clearly had. For Anna looked extremely startled, touched her forehead with one hand, turned and whispered something to Dan. When she turned back to the audience she was not smiling and seemed to Ned to be enclosing herself in some way, isolating herself. The audience was now silent. She nodded to Dan to begin the accompaniment. The Fauré songs were to open the program and during the prologue to the first one she closed her eyes.

Then at last her voice soared out and Ned himself felt the relief from tension she must be experiencing as she held together with her whole being the sustained line, without the slightest tremor. Ah, Ned was thinking, she has been learning . . . she has grown in a year. He was afraid the audience might applaud after the first song, but she quelled a small ripple with a glance and went right into the second one. And when the three songs were finished and the applause burst out, she gave Ned a dazzling smile much to his delight. So, after all, his being there had only thrown her for a second. And now he could simply enjoy.

The *Kindertoten lieder* were next. Anna had not left the stage and rather quickly created her silence. This is her element, Ned was thinking, this grave poignant music, and he was lost in its beauty when all of a sudden someone with a flash bulb stood up and began to take pictures. *"Augenblicke! O Augen!"* Anna's voice was just coming to a climax there, and broke. She walked to the apron, and Ned knew how angry she was because her eyes were black.

"Whoever has chosen to attack and destroy these exquisite Mahler songs with a flash bulb will please desist!"

Good, Ned thought, she is in control. But then she did not, could not leave it at that apparently.

"People who feel no reverence for music should not come to concerts. You can have no idea what such an interruption does to me, to the singer, as well as to the composer. You might as well have hurled an egg!"

"She's going a bit far," the woman sitting next to Ned whispered. "After all . . ."

"We'll begin again," Anna walked back to the piano, nodded to Dan who was wiping his face with a handkerchief and quickly put it back into his pocket. The silence was now very loud. We won't know, Ned was thinking, whether Anna has lost or won till the end of the songs.

Anna bowed her head for a few seconds, then looked out, far out above the heads of the audience and began the song again. When she came to *"Augenblicke! O Augen! O Augen!"* the tone was amazingly delicate and gentle. Anna had tears in her eyes, Ned saw with amazement, and from there the song rose in a long lament, as though all the anger had been transposed into this supremely disciplined art. That is what she could do, poise herself in the midst of acute conflict, and from there sing, he said to himself, like an angel.

The mystery of it! The strange being who could contain all this and give it out, who could be so passionate in her attack—and then so gentle. What was it all about? He hardly heard the next song he was so absorbed in what was happening to Anna herself. When the tempestuous last song ended, the applause broke out and seemed warm enough. The woman with the camera who had a center seat, pushed her way out and left the hall. Heads turned to watch her go while Anna was still acknowledging the applause. Then she and Dan walked off together.

A brief intermission, the program stated, would be followed by a performance of a Chopin etude by Dan before Anna's singing of two Mozart arias and the Brahms *Seri-*

ous Songs. Technically, Ned knew, this was the hardest part of the program. Should he go backstage now? No, he decided not to disturb her. She was still angry or in tears he imagined. It really had been a stroke of bad luck to be so startled out of a song, and Ned did not blame her for having been upset. But . . .

He was aware of a buzz of conversation all around him and decided to go out into the lobby and find out what the atmosphere was. The first thing he heard was a stout woman with flaming red hair saying loudly to a small knot of women around her, "Just plain arrogant! Poor Susie just adores her . . . she didn't mean any harm!"

"But it was an awful shock . . . " a gentler voice murmured. "People are so unaware . . . "

"I feel it was too bad. . Easterners come to Dallas and think we are savages . . . and now Susie did behave without thinking in quite a savage way!"

"Savage, my dear? Come now," said the woman with red hair. "Aren't you going a bit far?"

Ned moved to another part of the lobby, aware that people were looking at him and no doubt wondering what he was doing there. He leaned against the wall and surveyed the crowd. Well, he thought, Anna had certainly stirred them up!

"It's an amazing voice," an older woman was saying. "It reminds me of Kathleen Ferrier."

"But Ferrier would never have made such an outburst!"

"Who knows? Katharine Hepburn stopped the whole show when she was singing *Coco,* went right out on the stage and asked the person with a camera to leave the theater—and she got away with it!"

Ned devoured this last statement . . . I can tell Anna that when I go backstage.

"It's too bad," another woman interrupted, "it's sort of broken the spell, hasn't it?"

"You can't blame Anna Lindstrom for that! Susie Dennis should have known better!" The older woman seemed quite cross now. "You have no idea, apparently, of the concentration it requires to sing like that . . . or to give what Lindstrom gives . . . did you see the tears in her eyes?" At that moment the warning bell resounded and they all poured back into the auditorium.

Ned knew by the way Anna sailed onto the stage after Dan's very sensitive playing of Chopin that she was challenging herself and the audience at the same time, that she was going into the second half of the program determined to surpass herself. Ned remembered that she had told him once that Caruso felt the audience was the enemy and he must go in and kill it like a bull . . . the image had not registered with Ned at the time. It had seemed farfetched. But he recognized it now in the way Anna bowed without smiling at the flutter of applause, and in the way she lifted her head. Not triumph, her whole stance suggested, but attack. The audience responded with absolute attention.

How does one attack through Mozart? It soon became clear that an artist such as Anna attacks by giving a superlative performance. There was no power in her voice except the power of interpretation, except the flawless purity of her tone. It was as though the emotion back of the notes only made it possible for her to project with a greater exactness what Mozart had written. She was absolutely concentrated and Ned thought "Bravo, Anna!" He was suddenly immensely proud of her.

Through the Brahms songs he was again able to give himself up to the music and to recapture his own enjoyment, oblivious now of the audience, alone with Anna's voice, with her beautiful presence. They haven't been able to spoil it, he thought. This is why I came. Not to be near Anna but to see her at a distance, to hear her sing, to find myself in her world, the world where she can be wholly herself and at the same time the servant of music. Not love, not passion inhabited Ned now, but a strange peace.

He was startled out of it by the thunderous applause
and a few shouts of "Bravo" as Anna quickly left the stage,
aware no doubt that she would be called back again and
again, as indeed she was. The shouts were now "Encore!
Encore!" For a second she hesitated, smiling and making
deep bows, then she brought Dan out and sang Poulenc's
brief delightful *"Carpe"* and left the stage finally in a
ripple of laughter and applause.

Ned pushed his way backstage as fast as he could. She
was still in the wings, surrounded by women, but when
she saw Ned, she ran to him.

"Oh Ned!" The tone was one of despair, "Oh Ned, I
wanted to be wonderful, for *you*—and then I went and
wrecked it all."

"You were marvelous, Anna. You know you were."

"Really? Do you really think so?" She was looking him
straight in the eye.

"Yes," he said.

"But that awful woman!"

"I know, she should be shot at dawn." And at last Anna
laughed and hugged him hard.

"Oh Ned . . . " Then aware that they were surrounded,
she turned to the president, "Mrs. Ware, I want you to
meet my husband, Ned Fraser."

"You must be proud of her," Mrs. Ware shook his hand.
"You'll join us for lunch, I trust?"

"I'm afraid not. My plane leaves in an hour."

"Too bad you can't stay. Do you have to go back? You
could change your flight."

"I don't know how he got away," Anna said.

"Are you a doctor?" Mrs. Ware asked, trying to imagine,
no doubt, what profession he was in that would permit
such a trip.

"No, I fiddle around at a bank."

"He's president," Anna intervened. "You know how
Bostonians talk!"

"I really must go, Anna . . . " Ned was uncomfortable, out of place, and fled, leaving her to the tender mercies of the ladies. He wanted to keep what he had come for, Anna Lindstrom singing, keep it safe from the social amenities, keep it for himself alone.

Chapter XVII

At last, after the longest day, for it had seemed to Anna through the interminable luncheon and the interminable flight that she would never get home, at last she was in bed, lying in the crook of Ned's arm, like an exhausted swimmer back on earth.

"It's after midnight. We must get some sleep," she murmured.

"Let's talk," Ned said. Had he ever said any such thing before? "It's going to take a while for the buzz to die down, isn't it?"

"Yes."

Having expressed the wish to talk, Ned was silent, as though waiting for something to come to the surface. He slid his hand into hers and held it tightly.

"I'll never never get over seeing you there in that audience—seeing your face."

"Still crazy after all these years!" He laughed. "I was afraid for a moment I had thrown you off."

"Only for a second."

"Anna," Ned was looking up at the ceiling, his eyes wide open. "On the plane I was with my father."

"How do you mean?"

"Something helpless that needs help, the terrible in us . . . was that what you said?"

"I said it about anger . . . it's something Rilke said, actually."

"Never mind. On the plane I let my father in. I thought about him, not myself. Oh Anna . . . " it was wrenched out and Anna held very still. "I mourned my father."

"Something helpless," she turned it over in her mind.

"Somehow I got in touch with the person he never could let out . . . you did it, Anna. You made it happen."

"If only he could have done it—while he was alive."

"Oh no, the vulnerability was too great. He couldn't." Was Ned aware as Anna was that he was so connected with his father that he was now actually talking about himself? "If he once let the woe in he would not have been able to stop it . . . "

"But you've let the woe in," Anna whispered. "Thank God."

"Have I? Is that what this is all about?" Ned sat up and turned to look at Anna, a straight long look.

"Don't look at me like that, it makes me cry."

He lay down again and Anna asked, "Why did you come to Dallas, Ned? It was so strange—you could have thought about your father here, after all? Did it need a plane to Dallas?"

"I don't know. It was all connected in some way, you, my father—I had to hear you sing the *Kindertoten lieder* . . . I wasn't in a very rational state, I have to admit."

"Something happened when we had that talk—to me, too. I felt released. I went to Dallas free of my usual panic."

"What did happen, Anna?"

"My enemy had become my friend," the words jumped out. She had not realized the immensity of the change, but now she knew, and so she was able to say, "You were there and I wanted so much to be marvelous, to sweep you off your feet, and then I went and ruined it."

"You recovered, you did, Anna."

"I carried on, but you see I had let myself get in the way

of the music. The recovery was only a kind of assault. I forced those last songs."

"You're so honest, Anna." Ned realized as she said it, that she was right. It had been a triumph of will, of a kind of force in her, determined to win. "You did stun them, though, in the end."

"I got the applause, but no one was really moved. And that was my fault."

"Well, that flash-bulb carrying woman could be blamed, too."

"If you hadn't been there, maybe I could have handled it. I wanted something too much. I wanted to dazzle you, so I lost my balance when something beyond my control went wrong. That's bad," she said, smiling now, "But, oh Ned, it's such a comfort that I can talk like this to you now, without any defenses."

Fonzi, at the foot of the bed, groaned in his sleep, then gave a muffled bark.

"He's chasing a rabbit," Ned said, "the dear old dog."

Anna suddenly sat up, and for a second Ned wondered whether she was suffering one of those inexplicable changes of mood and was about to attack him.

"What's the matter?" he asked sharply.

"Darling, don't be afraid. I've just thought of something."

"You forgot to send the laundry out?" he teased, and sat up so they were face to face.

"No. I've got hold of something that has haunted me for ages. It was always there after a fight—something lost I could not lay my hands on."

"What was it?"

"Jacob and the angel—every time we fought, it was so painful because what we fought about was deeper than we could understand. I always knew that, but I didn't know how to come to grips with it."

"I'm at sea," Ned said, trying to read her face.

"Jacob didn't know who he was fighting or why . . . all I remember is that they fought till daybreak and the angel had wounded Jacob near the end. Then Jacob said, 'I will not let thee go, unless thou bless me.' "

"There didn't seem to be a blessing in those terrible fights. Only pain."

"Yes, pain, because the anger was a war to break through, a rage for withheld truth. Ned, Ned, can't you see? My anger was outrage at being shut out and yours was the fear of being found out, of being vulnerable. We had to get to the bottom of it—and we did when you talked about your father and cried, and the anger and the grief were all wrapped up together. I can't explain it," Anna said, lying down, her eyes closed. "But I felt the blessing. It has changed everything."

Ned thought this over. He was amazed at Anna's ability to say things in words. He was almost convinced. "But," he had to be clear, "do you really believe you'll never be furious with me again, or I with you for that matter?"

"I guess there may be some pretty thick fights ahead," she said quite calmly, as though they would not matter. "We're not going to change completely, Ned, but something has changed. There is understanding now. That's all I know."

Ned looked down at her face, her mouth so gentle and vulnerable, one arm relaxed over her head and the hand lying open on her hair. Had he ever seen Anna at peace? It was a little scary, she seemed so far away now, so he leaned over and put his arms under her and kissed her very gently, then long and deeply until he ran out of breath, and she opened her eyes.

"That," she said, running a finger along his mouth, "was a metaphysical kiss."

"Oh," Ned was smiling, "was that what it was? Let's do it again, a thousand times."

And they did. And the light was left on.

Yet the next morning at breakfast while Ned was calmly reading *The Wall Street News* as usual, Anna observed him, and wondered whether the exaltation she had felt had been all her imagination, whether radical change had taken place, or whether, as so often before, she had accomplished some inward journey alone and only imagined that Ned was there. She could not resist asking, "After last night, after all we experienced last night, do you suppose you could manage to say it, Ned?"

"Say what?" he laid the paper down and looked at her over his Benjamin Franklin glasses in a totally impersonal way.

"Say you love me."

"Oh Anna, must you?" He picked up the paper again and disappeared behind it.

And she, who had been so at peace, she who knew she should not have asked the question yet so needed to hear the words, felt in that instant as though she had been struck by lightning, stunned, furious, black with rage so intense and helpless that for a second she wanted to throw herself out of the window. Anything to escape the violence of her feelings. Instead she rushed out into the kitchen and burst into tears.

Only much later after Ned had left and she had been lying on the unmade bed for some time, her eyes wide open, staring at the ceiling, did she begin as she had done so many times before to unravel the tapestry and weave it together again. She would never never understand why Ned could not give what every lover gives and wants to give. So she was bound to be affronted and hurt again and again. Why stay? Why stay knowing there would always be violence, tears, pain and—yes—outrage to be dealt with? Why stay knowing that Ned would not and could not accept her as she was and would always be? Why stay, unwilling to compromise and unable to yield?

Because the very thing that tears us apart binds us together, she told herself. We are locked into an unremitting struggle each to defend and preserve authentic being.

Yet last night . . . for an hour or more, the struggle came out into light, and they had rested in each other at last. And as long as that had happened, there was the possibility of growth. If we could only not each feel so threatened by the other, Anna sighed, If only . . .

But whoever thought love was easy? Or that people change? No, the tapestry gets torn again and again and then rewoven in the same pattern and perhaps as time goes on our skill at reweaving becomes a little wiser and more compassionate: pride and fidelity and love.

Anna realized finally that what had happened in the night was real and could not be denied. To deny it because of what had happened in the morning, the insoluble clash of temperaments, was childish.

When she took Fonzi out into the Public Gardens she had made peace with herself.